MASTER
SUCCESSFUL
PERSONAL
HABITS

MASTER SUCCESSFUL PERSONAL HABITS

Zig Ziglar

Foreword by Tom Ziglar

Published 2021 by Gildan Media LLC
aka G&D Media
www.GandDmedia.com

FIRST EDITION 2019
FIRST PAPERBACK EDITION 2021

Front cover design by David Rheinhardt of Pyrographx

Design by Meghan Day Healey of Story Horse, LLC

Library of Congress Cataloging-in-Publication Data is available upon request

ISBN: 978-1-7225-0531-8

10   9   8   7   6   5   4   3   2   1

Contents

Foreword

by Tom Ziglar

I am very excited to introduce you to *Master Success-ful Personal Habits*. I've had the privilege of grow-ing up with Zig Ziglar and seeing him as a father, a speaker, an author, and a person. I've met with many people that he impacted—many of today's leading speakers, authors, and business leaders. They are still being influenced by his messages, his wisdom, and his philosophy—his core statement that you can have everything in life you want if you'll just help other people get what they want.

That is more true today than ever. People need help and encouragement more than they ever have. All you have to do is check out the Internet, listen to the news, listen to people in the line at Starbucks, and you'll see how many are concerned about the future. They don't know what's up next. But the sim-ple truths of life that are found in this book are the things that make all the difference. It's about your relationships. It's about the way you see yourself, and it's about the goals that you set and the way you view the future.

These teachings are the summation of Dad's entire career, and I think you have to go back to the start to figure out how we ended up here. In his early life, he was in sales, and he really struggled in the beginning. Then a wise person named P.C. Merrill spoke to Dad and taught him some important principles.

After that, Dad's sales career took off. In fact, he was immediately recognized as one of the top salespeople in an organization of over 7,000. When that happens, no matter what business you're in, you immediately get elected to do training. So Dad's first start in training was in sales training—sharing with others the principles, ideas, techniques, and tactics that he had learned and applied that made him successful.

As Dad grew into this role, he realized this simple truth: you can take all the best skills in the world and put them on the wrong person, and it won't do any good. So as Dad developed, and he started to learn and see people's responses, he realized that the first thing you had to do was develop the person from the inside out.

The person needed to have character and integrity and discipline. They needed to be motivated. They needed to have a specific goal-setting plan in place so they could become the right kind of person. Then they had to have relationship skills so that they could work with others.

Once you have that person, you can give them the technical skills, and they can do and achieve just about anything. That's what this book is about. It's about understanding that while skills are critically important, it doesn't really matter unless the right person is employing those skills.

Dad had an amazing impact. His character was unquestioned. The impact that he had on other people's lives to help them become more, be more, do more, and have more is legendary, but it wasn't until he passed away in 2012 that we really understood the magnitude of his legacy.

We had over 13,000 comments on our Facebook page within twenty-four hours of the announcement. As people sent in a message or an email or a letter or a card, the story was almost the same. It was this: "You know, I heard Zig Ziglar, in 1978, or 1986, or 1994. I was in a room, and there were 10,000, 20,000 people. When it was over, I was inspired, and I wanted to meet him. So I stood in line for two hours, and when I finally got to him to get that autograph, it was like I was the only person in the room."

For me, that's such a powerful story, because it's going to be hard for anybody to think, "Golly, I could be Zig Ziglar on stage," but you know what? I believe that each person reading this can be Zig Ziglar one-on-one. That means that you can give somebody undivided attention and let them know that you care about them.

My good friend Scott Schilling came to me and said, "Tom, I was backstage with your Dad years ago, and I asked him, 'Zig, how come when you speak to a large audience like this, 80 or 90 percent of your talk is exactly the same talk that you gave the last time?'" Scott said, "You know, Tom, your dad just smiled and looked at me, and he said, 'Scott, the truth never changes.'"

Dad went on to tell me many times that people are always hungry for the truth. I think that this book is more relevant today than ever, because for some reason our culture has bought into the idea that things are relative. Dad couldn't have disagreed more, and neither can I.

Things are more dependent upon the truth than ever. We want truth. We want to know that we can count on somebody. We want to deal with people who have honesty and integrity. We want to know that what we stand for and who we locks arms with have values that line up with truth.

As you go through this book and learn these different truths, understand that the more you employ them, the more effective you will be. Our good friend Seth Godin talks about the idea of trust. In his business, he focuses on scaling trust. Think about that—

scaling trust—because Dad said years ago that the number-one reason that people won't buy is lack of trust.

If we can build trust, then we've overcome the number-one objection that people have to us or to our product or service, and trust is the by-product of integrity. Many people ask, "What is Ziglar up to these days? Is Ziglar going to continue on?" and I am excited to say that Ziglar is about legacy.

Legacy really means this: it's the sum total of the impacts that you've had and the generational impacts that these have in turn, and so on and so on. Dad's legacy is living and growing even as we speak, as people are equipped with these materials and these ideas, use them in their own lives, and then teach others.

Dad's legacy lives on when we share these messages with others. That's why I'm so excited about this project, because it's not just a product with a result that ends some day. It's actually carrying on a legacy.

Legacy is different from *inheritance*. *Inheritance* is when you give somebody money or something like that which they can spend. *Legacy* is when you give somebody a guideline, a set of rules, a set of beliefs and principles that they can apply to any situation they go into and have it bear fruit. It's the difference between giving somebody a fish and teaching them how to fish.

Dad's legacy can be summed up in his famous quote, "You can have everything in life you want if you'll just help enough other people get what they want." There's pushback today in our society, because you hear about people who teach ideas of "win at all costs" or "crush the competition" or "in it to win it."

What does that mean in terms of Dad's legacy? First off, Dad believed, and I believe as well, that you want to start with having the other person's best interests in mind. When you serve somebody else's best interests first, and they know that, that builds a feeling of trust and endearment. Whether you can help them in that situation or not—the timing may or may not be right—they will always remember that. Over time business will seek you out, because people want to do business with people they know, like, and trust.

Legacy is a journey, and we all go through a journey in life. When I speak to organizations, I talk about the process we go through from survival to stability, from stability to success, and from success to significance. The world is hung up on this idea of success. This is a good thing; it's not a bad thing to say, "I want success," but success is really about the things you can have. It's about money or fame or influence, but people who understand the difference between success and significance are the ones who really get it.

Significance is when you help somebody else be, do, or have more than they thought possible. Legacy

is about significance. Again, it's about helping someone else become, be, do, or have more than they
thought possible. When you achieve significance,
you achieve the greatest level of joy imaginable,
because there is no greater joy than seeing somebody do something they didn't think they could
do. They look up, and they give you that smile, and
that's what drove Dad.

That's what inspires us today. It's to achieve not
only success but significance, and the more we seek
significance, the more likely we are to be successful
along the way.

Legacy is intentional. It's actually a choice, just as
attitude is a choice, or success is a choice; so, really, is
anything that we do.

There's a feeling today that "life is so full of circumstances. I have no control over where I'm going."

The reality is, you have complete control over
the choices you make. You may not like the circumstances, but you can choose to respond or react to
those circumstances, and Dad knew full and well
early on that he was going to leave a legacy.

You know what? You're going to leave a legacy
as well. The question is, what kind of legacy are you
going to leave? What kind of markers and mileposts?

Quick story on this. I had the job of helping Dad
clean out his library when he moved from his large
home to a smaller place in his last few years. As we
looked at those 3,000 books there, I knew I had to get
them down to about 100. Boy, that was a big task. I

had to decide which books I was going to keep and which we were we going to get rid of.

I decided to flip through each book. The more markings a book had in it, the more likely I was to save it in that special pile. As I was flipping through the books, I looked down, and I could see from his markings on a certain page that this was the foundational information that he used for part of one of his talks. It was like finding buried treasure, and when I closed the book—you wouldn't believe this—the title of the book was *Buried Treasure* by Rabbi Daniel Lapin.

So what kind of legacy are you going to leave? What kind of mileposts and markers will you leave behind when your kids go to your home or your office or your desk and flip through the books and look at your emails and texts? What kind of markers are you leaving?

Dad influenced my life in many ways, but he never said, "Son, I want you to be a speaker. I want you to follow in my footsteps and lead this company or be in sales."

I'm sure he hoped those things, but what he told me was this: "Son, whatever you do, I want you to do it with 100 percent effort and 100 percent integrity." That gave me the freedom to go out and explore who God made me to be. So, as you learn from this book, and you think about how you can impact those around you, I encourage you to take those words and realize that you are blessed with an incredible family and teammates and people that you associate with. Look for the best in them.

Dad gave me a set of philosophies, guidelines, truths to live by. It didn't matter what field of work I chose to go in. I knew that the right way to do it was with honesty and character and integrity, with hard work and discipline. When you add those to anything, success is far more likely and eventually will happen.

Dad was known for his book *See You at the Top*. In fact, if you do a Google search online and you read a list of the most influential personal development books of the last 100 years, that book will often be in the top ten. It impacted so many people.

Seth Godin says that we no longer live in the information age or the computer age; we live in the connection age. If you're going to live to win, you have to know how to employ the best ways to go forward in life, and that's by using these foundational principles and truths. With all the changes that happen before our eyes every day, these truths never change.

This book contains a lot of references to personalities of the mid-1990s, such as sports figures, celebrities, and politicians. These personalities aren't in the foreground of people's attention these days, but the lessons they embody continue to live on.

Some people are saying that Dad's ideas are kind of old-school, that they don't really apply to today's world. I couldn't disagree more.

People may be good marketers. They may know how to write good headlines, things that'll catch people's attention, and I applaud them for that, but here's the reality. Dad said there were some absolutes. For example, would you hire an accountant to work for your company who was *relatively* honest? Of course not. That's a truth that never changes.

There are relationship principles that never change. The ways people like to be talked to and respected never change. These are the core, foundational things that we talk about.

So when you look at how you're going to carry forward in life, are you going to try the new guru on the street, or are you going to look to the wisdom of the ages? After all, why do they call it the wisdom *of the ages*?

When I first started working at the company over twenty-eight years ago, I heard Dad tell our team, "We're not in the book and tape business. We're in the life-changing business." As you read this book, you might see Dad talk about tapes and books and other things that now are available electronically and digitally, on your iPhone or in the cloud. He'll also talk about the value of listening to the tapes. Know this: it's not the medium that makes a difference, it's the message. And you can absorb the message by reading just as well as by listening.

This material is more relevant than ever, because now more than ever, you can see how the people who embrace these ideas stand out. That's right. When you employ these ideas, you become rare. You become a leader. You become an example. And you have a competitive advantage, because unfortunately today these principles are not commonly taught anywhere, unless you seek them out on your own—and that's what you are doing by reading this book.

Tom Ziglar is the president of Ziglar Training Corporation, the author of the book *Live to Win*, and a successful platform speaker in his own right.

CHAPTER

Four Concepts That Make a Difference

I'm Zig Ziglar, and I want to begin by saying this book is for everyone. Whether you're a mechanic or a physician, whether you're a college professor or a kindergarten student, you will benefit from this information.

Let me say simply that this is also about hope. Psychologist Alfred Adler said that hope is the foundational quality of all change. It's my conviction that encouragement is the fuel of that hope, and so this material is designed to encourage and inform. Countless adults have shared with me that these concepts have had a dramatic influence in their lives.

Below I will give you an idea that you will agree is absolutely significant. Then I will give you four concepts that, if you will apply them, will make a difference in your life. As I present them to you, you're going to be thinking, "You know, I like that. I'm going to remember it."

When you finish this material, virtually none of you will be able to give all four of them back to me. That's why we will encourage you to expose yourself to this over and over: because repetition is the mother of learning. That makes it the father of action, and that means it's the architect of accomplishment.

Now let's start with this. Do you honestly and sincerely believe that there's something you can specifically do in the next two weeks that would make your personal life, your family life, and your business life all *worse*?

You probably know the next question then. Do you believe there's something you can specifically do that will make all of them *better*? OK.

Do you believe that the choice is yours? Do you believe that every choice has an end result? Do you believe making the right choices is your responsibility?

Probably you've said yes to these questions. Now here's what you have said, whether you realize it or not. You have just said that regardless of how good or bad my past has been, regardless of how good or bad my present is, there is something I can specifically do now that will make my future either better or worse, and the choice is mine.

Now, folks, that's profound. I'll always tell you when I've said something profound, because I found out a few years ago that an incredibly high percentage of people do not recognize my profound statements when I make them unless I tell them they are profound.

This is going to involve a lot of communication. A lady once went to see her attorney about a divorce. The lawyer said, "What's the problem?"

She started rambling.

He said, "No, be specific."

She said, "Like how?"

"Well, do you have any grounds?"

"Oh, yes, as a matter of fact, we have about forty acres right out here on the north end of town."

"No, that's not what I'm talking about. Do you have a grudge?"

"No, but we have a really neat little carport right on the side of the house."

"Woman, we need to make this personal."

"Like how?"

"Well, does that man ever beat you up?"

"Oh, no, I'm up every day at least an hour before he even turns over."

The lawyer said, "Do you accept any responsibility for the difficulty?"

The woman said, "Like how?"

"Well, for example, do you ever wake up grouchy?"

"Oh no, I just let him get up on his own whenever he will."

"Well, why do you want to divorce the man?"

"The guy just can't communicate."

We're going to try to make this communication such that as you read this book, you will have no difficulty understanding exactly what I am talking about. Everything is choice. For example, for twenty-four years of my adult life, by choice I weighed well over 200 pounds. The reason I say "by choice" is simply because I have never *accidentally* eaten any-thing. It's always been a choice. If I choose to eat too much, then I have chosen to weigh too much. You are where you are because of a series of choices that you have made.

I'm the tenth of twelve children. I asked my mom one time, "Mom, why so many?" She said, "Well, son, where do you think I should have stopped?" It's for sure that I didn't think it was after number nine: you can absolutely count on that.

Let me say something that I think is very import-ant. A few minutes ago, you made the observation that the responsibility was yours to make the right choices. Responsibility carries a lot of weight in life.

Barbara Tuchman, a two-time Pulitzer Prize win-ner, said the number-one need we have in our society today is for people to accept responsibility. That is so tremendously true.

I was raised during the Depression. My dad died when I was five years old. There were six of us who were too young to work. Yazoo City—a small Missis-sippi town. We don't even have a village drunk; we share him with a little community next to us. But it's exciting about once a month when a train comes through. I know that doesn't sound like excitement until I explain we don't have tracks there. We used to hang a mirror at the end of Main Street to make the town look bigger.

I can joke about my home town for one very good reason. It's an amazing little town.

The former president of the American Medical Association is from Yazoo City. The former president of the American Bar Association is from Yazoo City. The former president of the Southern Baptist Convention is from Yazoo City. The former editor of *Harper's Magazine* is from Yazoo City. So are the former secretary of agriculture and the chairman of the Republican Party. Comedian Jerry Clowers is from Yazoo City.

The point I'm making there is that we can joke about that little town because of its productivity. People who are confident and productive don't mind you kidding them along.

In any case, I don't need to tell you that we had a tough time financially. Other families had it tough too, but I'm grateful that for whatever reason, I did not choose to notice what we did not have.

I did notice what a lot of people *did* have in that little town. Even in those times, I noticed that some people wore nice clothes. They drove nice cars. They lived in nice houses. They took nice trips. They even had dinner out. Some of them even played golf at the country club.

I've noticed that there are some people that don't pay any attention at all to the economy, regardless of how it is. (As you know, the media has accurately predicted twenty-seven of the last two recessions.)

Now there are some people who just don't pay any attention to what other people are doing. For example, I've noticed that in some instances, many instances, when the economy is absolutely magnificent, there are a bunch of folks going broke. I have noticed that in some instances where the economy is absolutely horrible, there are a bunch of folks getting rich.

Major point number one is, you do have a choice. You can do something now about your life, making it better or worse, and the choice is here.

Point number two is this: it is not what happens out there that makes a difference in your life. A lot of that you cannot change. There's nothing you can do about Bosnia personally at this moment. There *is* something you can do about you and your future. It's what goes on between your own two ears. That's what makes the difference.

Neil Rudenstine is the president of Harvard University. His mother is a part-time waitress. His father is a prison guard. This is point number three. It's not who your mama and your daddy might have been. It's not what they have done. The question is what kind of legacy you will leave to your children and your grandchildren. It is what *you* do.

A lot of times we encounter people who have a pity party on a regular basis. They have what we call the PLOM disease, P-L-O-M. That's "poor little old me." The problem with pity parties is that when they have them, very few people come, and those who do don't bring presents.

They did a study of 300 world-class leaders. I'm talking about Roosevelt and Churchill. I'm talking about Martin Luther King and Mahatma Gandhi. I'm talking about Clara Barton and Helen Keller and Mother Teresa, world-class leaders, 300 of them. Seventy-five percent of them were either raised in poverty or had been abused as children or had some serious physical impairment.

They understood point number four: it's not what happens to you, it's how you handle what happens to you that is going to make the difference. I think, for example, of the Edsel automobile, which many people recognize as being by far the most profitable motor car that Ford ever built.

I know what you're thinking right now: "Ziglar, that sucker was a dog. It cost them a whole lot of money. They stopped production. What do you mean it was the most profitable one?"

Remember—it's not what happens to you, it's how you handle it. You see, out of the Edsel came the Mustang. Out of the Mustang came the Taurus. They took the mistake, learned from it, capitalized on it, and look at what happened as a result. It's not what happens to you. It's how you handle it.

John Foppe was recognized two years ago as one of the top ten young Americans by the United States Junior Chamber of Commerce. I met John when he was speaking for the Department of Defense up in Colorado Springs. He had admirals, generals, CEOs of the Fortune 500 companies in front of him. He was a nineteen-year-old man, and he spoke with confidence and clarity and conviction and power.

John graduated from college cum laude in three and a half years, working his way partially through. You ought to see John drive a car and scramble eggs and go skiing and paint portraits. You ought to watch him just eat. You see, John Foppe was born without any arms.

John said to me one day, he said, "You know, Zig, if I had the longest, strongest arms ever put on a human being, he said there'd still be only so high I could reach, only so much weight I could lift. I don't care how long and tall and strong and big your arms might be, they have a limit, but I face more situations every day where I have to use my creative imagination than the average person does in a month's time. There's no limit to what we can do internally."

The message is the power of hope, because if there's hope in the future, there is power in the present.

My objective here is to share how you can get more of the things that money will buy and all of the things that money *won't* buy.

Money is important. At least in one or two instances in our lives, all of us have been in situations where if we had a flat tire, it was a financial disaster. If we spilled something on a dress or tore a suit, it really represented difficulty. We would run out of gas on the highway. There are people you know who are struggling for survival.

Part of my objective is to help those people. We want to share with you how to move from survival to stability. Then how do you move from stability to success, and then how do you move from success to significance? Money is important. Don't misunderstand: it's not everything, but it ranks reasonably close to oxygen. It has to be in the picture. Anybody says they're not interested in money is going to lie about other things too.

I have to confess, I like the things that money buys. I like to wear nice clothes. I like to drive a nice car. I like to live in a nice house. I like to take nice trips. I like to take my wife out to nice restaurants. I *like* all of those things, and all of them cost money, but I *love* the things money won't buy. Money bought me a nice house. It'll never buy me a home. Money will buy me a bed. It won't buy me a good night's sleep. Money will buy me a companion. It won't buy me a friend. Money will buy me a good time, but it won't buy peace of mind. All of those things are available. I'll never tell you it's easy, but they are available.

I want to share with you how you achieve job security in a world where job security no longer exists. How do you live well, and how do you finish well? How do you develop the qualities that are necessary to accomplish all of these things, and do you have what it takes?

I'm going to be giving you a lot of stories, examples, and illustrations. The Center for Creative Leadership out of Greensboro, North Carolina, said that the parable, the story, and the example are the best way to teach, particularly if you're teaching values. Seems that a couple of thousand years ago, somebody else used the parable quite effectively in teaching the truths that really do make a difference.

As you read this, you might be wondering, "You know, Zig, you've said some pretty significant things about what is available. I wonder"—poor little old me, PLOM disease in full force—"can *I* accomplish those things?"

Let me tell you about Vince Robert, and you see how you compare to Vince. How old are you? He's thirty-seven years old. How much education do you have? He had a fifth-grade education. What do you do? He drove a taxi.

Where do you think Vince Robert was going to end up, in the minds of a lot of people? Many would say that there's a perfect candidate for governmental assistance, but one day when Vince was waiting on a fare in front of a hotel, lightning struck.

Vince Robert bought a book. It was a dictionary, a fifteen-pound Webster's dictionary.

He put that dictionary on the front seat of his automobile, and starting on word one, page one; he started learning those words. By the time he had barely gotten into the dictionary, maybe an eighth of an inch into it, all of a sudden he started understanding things he'd only been hearing, understanding things he'd only been reading.

This has been validated by Georgetown Medical School, whose studies said that in 100 percent of the cases, no exception, when your vocabulary increases, your IQ goes up. You can build a magnificent vocabulary and not invest any time at all. All you have to do is get a dictionary and put it in the bathroom.

Now let me tell you what happened to Vince Robert. As he started hearing things and listening to things, he started understanding them. He started investing in the stock market, took every dime he could spare. He ended up buying the 19 Car Cab Company. He kept investing. Today he's a wealthy man and travels through Canada telling people how he did it.

You know what I believe with all my heart? There are tens of thousands of Vince Roberts who will listen to what I just said and say, "If that guy can do it, I can do it too." That's what this is all about.

I want to share with you a basic concept which you will hear me repeat over and over: failure is an event. It's not a person. Yesterday really did end last night. Today really is a brand-new day, and it gives us another choice to do with it whatever it is that we wish to do.

One thing I'm going to be covering is, how do you get along with other people? How do you get along with that bloodsucker of a boss who wants to squeeze every ounce of blood out of you and only pays you minimum wage because it's the law? How do you get along with that lazy, irresponsible employee who wants all the benefits and does none of the work? They think they ought to show up when they want to, where they want to, how they want to, and do what they want to. How do you get along with that person? How do you get along with that man you're married to that no human being alive could ever tolerate? How do you get along with that woman? How do you handle that irresponsible, lazy teenager? How do you get along with all of these people?

Let me tell you how you handle a job you hate. I was going through the airport out at Dallas–Fort Worth, the security bit. This young man was there. I always say, "Thank you very much. How are you doing?" He said, "Just awful. I hate this job." I smiled at him, and I said, "That's interesting. I'm certain that there are thousands of people in Dallas alone who would love to have this job that you absolutely hate."

The young man did a quick double-take and said, "You know, I never thought about that."

I said, "Well, don't you really think you ought to think about it just for a moment?"

How do you learn to love a job that you hate? If you can't learn to love it, how do you get to be productive?

Let me tell you a story about a guy named Richard Oates. Richard Oates was a superintendent with one of the nation's largest homebuilders. For five years he worked with them. The last three years he was under such intense pressure that he told me less than a week ago, he said, "You know, I hated Sundays." I said, "Why on earth did you hate Sundays?" He said, "Because Sunday was the last day before I would have to get back in the rat race, and I was under so much pressure, I was stressed out to an incredible degree."

Let me tell the rest of that story. In the five years he was there, he only missed four days because of illness. In the last three years he was there, he was never late a single time regardless of the weather, regardless of how he felt, regardless of car trouble. He never used his complete vacation time. The last year he was there, he was recognized as one of their top superintendents. He would have undoubtedly gotten the award for being the best, but in the meantime he had accepted a better position, and they certainly don't give those awards to people when they have left the company.

Perhaps the most amazing thing, though, is that although he had 400 home units that he was in charge of, with fifteen to twenty homes going up at all times, in the last ten months he built and closed eighty-three homes without missing a single move-in date. That is absolutely unbelievable.

I asked him, "How did you do it?" He said, "Well, first of all, there is a question of survival. I do have responsibilities. I just love to eat. I have a responsibility to my wife. I have other responsibilities. I had a responsibility to my company. I'm known as a company man. My responsibility was to give them the very best that I had regardless of how I might be feeling at the moment."

Now, folks, that's what we call character. Character is the ability to carry out a good resolution long after the excitement of the moment has passed. That is accepting responsibility. He also said, "I had a mentor, Stan Sermanack, who had taken me under his wing and made it possible for me to get this particular job. He was my mentor and encourager. I did not want to let him down."

What is all of that saying? There are some absolutes in life. We talk about relative this and relative that, but as far as I'm concerned, relatives are brothers and sisters and in-laws, but there are values that are not relative. Suppose we were to take the laws and say, "We have about 2,000 on the books. I believe in this one and this one, but I don't like that one at all. I'm going to take that one out of there." We would be in chaos, would we not? It would be anarchy.

Now the thing I like best of all about Richard Oates—and I recognize that this is going to sound a little self-serving—is that he happens to have married one of the most beautiful girls I've ever seen in my life: my daughter. That means that he's my son-in-law, but today he's also our vice-president in charge of marketing and product development, applying the same energy, the same commitment. He took a job he did not like, gave it his absolute best, and learned the skills, the commitment, the responsibility to move into a better job. Don't like your job? Give it your best shot. That's the way you get a better job.

Let me give you another illustration. My executive assistant, Laurie Majors, is quite a story. She's been with me eighteen years. She finished the tenth grade. Two years ago, we evaluated our key employees. Laurie graded out at slightly above the master's degree level. You can finish school. You can even make it easy. You never finish your education, and it is seldom easy. She simply keeps on learning, keeps on going.

Anyway, Laurie got a phone call from this lady in Birmingham, Alabama. After the call, she said to me, "You know, Zig, the lady thinks she has an incredible problem. I think that you could probably solve it in five minutes if you can meet with her when you get to Birmingham." I said, "I'll get there early. Invite the lady to come backstage. We'll have a little chat."

Incidentally, I don't do counseling. I'm not trained for it. I don't have the time for it. My natural inclination is to believe everything from the last person I talked to, and that doesn't really make for professional counseling. If somebody says, "I have a problem," if I have five minutes, I'll give it my best shot. That's all I can do.

When the lady spotted me, she came walking across the stage, and I have never seen such anger in my life. I mean, the stage was rattling. I'm not going to say she was overweight, but she was about five and a half inches too short. She was the kind of lady that can brighten up a room by leaving it, if you know what I mean. When she saw me, she started crying,

"Oh, I'm so glad to see you. I've got this terrible job. I just hate it. I want out of it. Can you help me?"

Now I could imagine this lady thinking that I was going to verbally put my arm around her and say, "Yes, my dear. Life is tough, but you have to hang in there, and by and by things will work out OK." I could have done that, but if I had, I would have betrayed everything in which I believe. If somebody says, "Help!" I believe I'm supposed to help.

As I said, I don't do any counseling, but I'm fortunate to have access to some of the outstanding minds in this country. I check things out psychologically, physiologically, and theologically, and have strong endorsements from all three disciplines before I record it, write it, or verbalize it.

There's one thing I do know about counseling, and that is that most people who come to you with a problem do not want a solution to the problem. What they want is to tell you about it. They want to talk about the problem. They do not want to solve the problem. If you foul up the deal and solve the problem, then they can't tell you about again and again and again.

I had very few minutes. I knew I had to get her attention, so I said, "Yes, you know, ma'am, the sad thing is I believe your situation is about to get a whole lot worse." Had I hit her in the face with a bucket of ice water, I could not have stunned her more.

She said, "What do you mean?"

I said, "I believe that your company is going to fire you."

"Fire me? Why on earth would they fire me?" Isn't it the truth that people who are the problem never recognize they are the problem? They're in complete denial. They think denial is just a river in Egypt. No snowflake ever blames itself for the blizzard. No raindrop ever blames itself for the flood, but each plays a part. Every person in life either builds or tears down. "Why would they fire me?"

I said, "Ma'am, I don't believe there's a company in America big enough to sustain this much poison in one small spot."

All of a sudden the job she hated everything about took on a different hue. She said, "Well, what am I going to do?"

"Do you really want to know?" I said.

"Yes, that's the reason I came to you for help, but you sure haven't been much help so far."

"Well, ma'am, I've got an idea. I believe it'll work. If you will do it, I know it will work."

"Tell me about it."

"When you get home tonight, I want you to get a sheet of paper out, and I want you to make a list of all the things you do like about your company and the people down there."

She interrupted me. She said, "That'll be easy. I don't like nothing about that company. I don't like nothing about those people down there."

"Let me ask you a question. Do they pay you for working there?"

"Of course they pay me for working there."

"You don't like to be paid for working?"

"I certainly do."

"Then you like to be paid."

"Of course."

"Well, that's one thing you like about your job."

"Why, certainly."

"A minute ago you said there was nothing you liked about the job."

"I didn't know you was talking about that."

"Well," I said, "don't you think money's important?"

"Yes."

"OK, let me ask you the second question. Do they pay you above average, below average, or about average for what you do?"

"Well," she said, "I have to confess. They pay me above average."

"Don't you like to be paid above average?"

"Why, certainly I do."

"I'll tell you what I want you to do. I want you to get that sheet of paper out right now. We're going to make a list of all of the things that you do like about your job."

She just sat there. I said, "No, go ahead. Get paper out. We'll make a list right now." She just sat there. I said, "Ma'am, let me tell you what my experience in life has been. People that won't take step one never take step two. If you're unwilling to get involved in solving your own problem, we might as well terminate the interview. I can't solve your problem as you listen to this. I can give you some ideas, some information that will put you in better a position to solve it, but I cannot solve your problem, nor can anyone else. We can give you ideas and information, but ultimately the solution has to be there."

She didn't want any part of having to solve her problem, so I did that. I said, "You got your notebook in your hand. Open it up, and let's take some notes."

With anger, she opened the book. She said, "Now, what did you say the first thing I liked about my job was?"

"They pay you for working there. Write it down. 'I like my job.'"

By the time we got through, there were twenty-two things she liked about her job. She had three weeks' vacation with pay. She had hospitalization insurance, health insurance. She was on a profit-sharing plan, had a great retirement plan. She was on a bonus program. She was in on executive decisions. She lived less than fifteen minutes from her office—twenty-two things.

"Now, ma'am," I said, "when you get home tonight, I want you to get this list out. I want you to change it from 'I like my job because . . .' to 'I love my job.' I want you to get in front of the mirror, and I want you to look yourself right in the eye and say, 'I love my job,' and do it with enthusiasm. You'll sleep better tonight. When you get up tomorrow morning, get back in front of the mirror before you go to work, look yourself right in the eye, and say exactly the same thing. Take the list with you, because in twenty-four hours, you will have moved from being a fault-finder to a good-finder."

You know, a lot of people look for fault; they try to find fault as if there's a reward for it. I said, "You will begin to look for something good, and you'll be amazed at how much that list is going to grow. Do this every morning, every night for the next thirty days."

Six weeks later, I was back over there conducting a sales seminar. In the meantime, she had gotten our set of tapes, and she had learned that everybody's in sales. The sales department is not our company, but our whole company is our sales department. Everybody's in sales.

When I got there for the sales seminar, there she sat, right in the front row, grinning so wide she could have eaten a banana sideways. She was really excited. I said, "How are you doing?" She grinned even more broadly, and she said, "I'm doing wonderfully well, Mr. Ziglar. You cannot believe how much those people down there have changed."

How do you change all those people you're talking about? You don't. You change *you*. When you change you, that's when your world begins to change. God said to build a better world. I said, "How? It's such a cold and lonely place, and I'm so small and useless. There's nothing I can do," but God in all his wisdom said, "Just build a better you."

That's what this is about: building a better you, because you have to *be* before you can *do*; you have to *do* before you can *have*. You have such a wide range of choices, and we're filled with them.

There's a story of two twins. One of them was an alcoholic. One was enormously successful. In separate interviews, they asked the alcoholic twin, "How did it happen that you became an alcoholic?" He said, "I had no choice. My father was an alcoholic." They asked the successful young man, "How did you do it?" He said, "I had no choice. My father was an alcoholic. I didn't want to be like him." The choice, you see, is ours. We go through life with that.

I do tell a lot of stories. I want to share a lot of philosophy with you. Philosophy simply means the love of wisdom. One thing that you will hear me say over and over is that you can have everything you want in life if you'll just help enough other people get what they want.

I'll be quoting a lot of people. I'll be quoting John Maxwell, John Johnson, Solomon, Lincoln, Emerson, St. Augustine, Christ, Helen Keller, Mother Teresa, Dr. Forest Tennant, Rabbi Daniel Lapin, Martin Luther King. I'll quote Mahatma Gandhi, and many others. I try to give credit when somebody gives me information. I do that for three reasons. Number one, it is the right thing to do. Number two, it indicates I've done my research. Number three, if it's wrong, I can always say, "That fellow ought to have known better than that."

Let me say to you without any fear of error that you were born to win, but in order to be the winner that you were born to be, you have to plan to win. You have to prepare to win, and then and only then can you legitimately expect to win.

At Stanford University in 1920, Dr. Lewis Terman started a study on 1,440 gifted youngsters. When he retired, another professor was assigned to them. They followed them to the end of their lives. Many of them were extremely successful, brilliant young men and women. Many had gone on to great success. Not a single one attributed their success to their IQ. They attributed their success to their ability to focus on the issue at hand.

When a lot of people are working on the job, they're thinking about other things. They're thinking about their families. When they're with their families, they're thinking about their jobs, and they're not doing either job very effectively. You really need to be able to focus on what's going on.

You were born to win, but you have to plan, you have to prepare, and you have to expect to win. Bobby Knight, who has won three national championships in basketball at Indiana University, says that the will to win is nothing without the will to *prepare* to win.

I'm not a football expert, but I do know one thing about it: in the last two minutes of the half, and in the last two minutes of the game, they score 20 percent of all of the points that are scored during the entire sixty minutes.

In four minutes, they score 20 percent of all of the points in the entire sixty minutes. The reason they do is they have the two-minute offense. The end of the first half, the end of the second half is when they do the score, and they plan to score, they prepare to score, and consequently, they expect to score. Then, incredibly enough, the defense cooperates with them to help them score.

I know you're thinking now, "Ziglar, that's crazy, man. Why, the defense all week long practices that defense. They take the linebackers out, they send out their nickelbacks, they put in their two best pass rushers, they get in a bend but don't break mode. They call it their *prevent defense*."

Let me ask you a question. If they score three times as fast against the prevent defense as they do against the regular defense, is it prevent or permit? What do you think?

A few thousand years ago, a fellow named Job said something profound: "That which I feared greatly has come to pass." They're afraid they're going to score, and that fear comes to pass.

Psychologists will tell you in a New York minute— and for your information that's thirty-two seconds— that you move to the strongest impression in your mind. If you're afraid they're going to score on you, then the chances go up that, yes, they will score on you.

Did you know that if an arresting police officer keeps the light flashing when he pulls a motorist aside, the odds are seven times as great that he will be run into by passing motorists? That's right; they call it the *moth attraction*. The field-goal kicker that says, "Oh, I'll miss it, we'll lose the game," is much more likely to miss it than is the one that says, "I'll split the uprights, we'll win the game."

The worst possible thing a parent can say to a child who wants to help with the dishes is "OK, but be careful. This is our best china. Don't break it." If they had sat up all night praying, "Lord, what can I tell this kid to help him break the dishes?" they couldn't do a better job than that.

The sales manager who sends a salesperson out and says, "This is our number-one account, don't foul it up" couldn't have given a worse instruction. He should say, "I'm sending you out because I have complete confidence that you're the one person I can depend on to handle this in the best possible way."

Let me give you a specific example. How many of you remember the tragedy that took place in San Francisco in 1982 when the San Francisco 49ers beat the Dallas Cowboys in the NFL championship game? (I know a lot of you are not going to think that's a tragedy, but believe me, it was.)

Dallas had just gone ahead and scored a touch-down. Now they kicked off two minutes of play. Joe Montana led the 49ers all the way down the field. We had our prevent defense in there. You know what the play was. He sent Dwight Clark into the end zone. He threw him the pass. Clark jumped twenty-eight feet straight up in the air and made the catch, and the 49ers won the game.

The next day, Tex Schramm, who was the pres-ident of the Cowboys at that time, was being inter-viewed by the media. They asked him, "Tex, what happened?" He gave us a lesson in life with his answer. He said, "The Dallas Cowboys went out there determined not to lose the game. The San Francisco 49ers went out there determined to win the game."

I want you thinking, how do I win the game. From what I know about football (I'm not a football coach, but I am a verbal coach), I wouldn't send nickelbacks out there to defend for my team. I would send the Bruise Brothers out there. I would send the takeover guys. I would send the control team out there. I would send the intimidators out there. I would send some-body out determined not only to keep them from scor-ing, but to take that ball away and score ourselves.

Yes, I believe that you were designed for accom-plishment. I believe you were engineered for success. I believe you're endowed with the seeds of greatness. You were born to win, but you have to have a plan if you are going to win.

What is winning? The reality is that all of us want basically the same thing: Everybody wants to be happy. I've never met anybody who said, "I want to be miserable." Everybody wants to be healthy. Everybody wants to be at least reasonably prosperous, and I know many of you want to be *un*reasonably prosperous. That's OK. I've had money, and I haven't had it, and I'm here to tell you it's better to have it.

A lot of times my Bible-reading friends will misquote the Bible and say, "You know, Zig, the Bible says that money is the root of all evil," but it doesn't. It says the *love of* money is the root of all evil.

Two-thirds of Christ's parables had to do with our physical and financial well-being. Two-thirds of the success stories there had to do with that subject. There's a lot more talk about success in the Bible than there is about heaven. The Good Samaritan never could have put that old boy in the inn after he'd been mugged if he hadn't had some money to do it with.

Yes, everybody is interested in money. Everybody wants to be secure. They want to have friends and peace of mind, they want to have good family relationships, and they want to have hope that the future is going to be even better.

What part does hope play in all of this? I believe it's the basis of everything. You see, John Maxwell says if there's hope in the future, there's power in the present. Answer these questions.

How happy could you be if you had no hope? How healthy would you be if you had no hope? How prosperous could you be if you had no hope? How secure are you with no hope? How many friends would you be able to accumulate if you're the kind of person who's just always moping and groping and griping and complaining? How much peace of mind would there be, and how would your family relationships be?

I think hope is the key to an awful lot of things. Let me emphasize a point: I will never tell you that acquiring these things is going to be easy. I know that life is tough, but I also know that when you're tough on yourself, life can be tremendously rewarding to you.

When you discipline yourself to do the things you need to do when you need to do them, the day's going to come when you can do the things you want to do when you want to do them. My friends, the road to the top goes through lots of valleys. You do not develop champions on a featherbed. There have to be those trials and difficulties in order for you to develop the muscles and the qualities that are going to make a difference in your life. You have to *be* before you can *do*. You have to *do* before you can *have*.

CHAPTER 2

The Size of the Hope

Some years ago I was coming in on a plane, which is generally the way I fly, and I was seated next to an old boy. I couldn't help but notice he had his wedding band on the index finger of his left hand. I commented on it. I said, "Friend, you have your wedding band on the wrong finger." He said, "Yes, I married the wrong woman."

Well, I don't know if he married the wrong woman or not. I'm delighted to be able to say I did *not* marry the wrong woman. (When I talk about my wife, at her suggestion, I always call her the redhead. When I'm talking to her, it's sugar baby. Incidentally, her name is Jean.) You see, we had been married over twenty-seven years before I was ever able to give her financial stability, much less financial security.

Yet during all those years, not once do I ever remember her saying, "Honey, if we just had more money, here's what we could do," or, "If we had more financial stability, here's what we could do."

There was one five-year stretch when I was in seventeen different deals, and that's all they were, just deals. In all those years, she would always say, "Honey, tomorrow's going to be better. You can do it." Then, the two things that meant the most to me, "I love you, and I believe in you." I cannot begin to tell you what it meant to me to have a cheerleader cheering for me every day of my life and praying for me every night of my life.

I can tell you without any reservation that had it not been for her, I would not be talking to you right now. That encouragement and support meant it all. She knows, and I know about her, first of all, that half the money is hers. The only time she goes berserk is when she's shopping for the grandchildren. Had we known grandchildren were going to be so much fun, we certainly would have been nicer to their parents.

Anyhow, she knows that I delight in seeing her go shopping now, because she's very responsible. It's a delight to be able to have her do that, because for so long she could not. No, she does not get the least bit upset about the fact that I tease about that.

One reason I believe I'm qualified to make suggestions and make a difference in your life is that I've walked in your shoes. Today I was reminiscing about when I was a young salesman in Lancaster, South Carolina, and we were having such a struggle. I've had my lights turned off. I've had my telephone disconnected. I had to turn a car back in that I didn't want to turn back in.

My first baby was born. The hospital bill was $64. I didn't have $64. I had to get out and make two sales in order to get my own baby out of the hospital. I vividly remember one day as I was struggling with "How do I eat?" and "How do we put gasoline in the car to go make the sales calls?" I was going through some of my drawers there at home. There were two twenty-dollar bills and a ten-dollar bill, and it looked like all the money in the world.

I've been confused many times in my life. I didn't know what I'd be doing tomorrow, much less next week, next month, or five years down the path. I don't believe there's anybody who has ever been as despondent on occasion in those early years and as puzzled and as curious. "What do I do? Why can't I make things happen?" I've been down that route, and yes, I've hurt as much as anybody, I believe.

On May 13, 1995, my oldest daughter went home to be with the Lord. I know what it is to feel pain. I know what does work. I know what does *not* work, and that's the reason I believe hope is such an important ingredient.

John Maxwell put it well: "If there's hope in the future, there's power in the present." John Johnson put it this way: "It's not the color of your skin. It's not the place of your birth. It's the size of your hope that's going to determine where you're going to go in your life."

John Johnson was born in a shotgun house with a tin roof in Arkansas City, Arkansas. For those of you who don't know what a shotgun house is, let me simply tell you that it's so named because you could point a shotgun and fire it through that house and wouldn't hit anything at all, because it's just a shell.

Today John lives next door to Bob Hope part of the time. He lives in a high-rise on Chicago's Gold Coast overlooking Lake Michigan the rest of the time. He's been a guest in the White House with every president since Eisenhower. He's one of the 400 wealthiest people in America. He owns his own insurance company, his own cosmetics company, *Ebony* magazine. When he says it's not the place of your birth or the color of your skin, it's the size of the hope, I take him very seriously, because I do believe he knows what he is talking about.

If an individual really wants to be happy and healthy and prosperous and secure and have friends, peace of mind, good family relationships, and hope, let me tell you that you have to deal with all facets of life. You have to deal with your personal life, your family life, and your career. You cannot separate them.

The January 8, 1990, issue of *USA Today* said the number-one cause of productivity decline in America today is marital difficulty at home. You can't have a knockdown drag-out at home and go to the job and be as productive as you otherwise would be. You cannot get fired or chewed out by the boss on the job and go home with the same attitude as you'd have if you had just been given a significant raise or recognition. You cannot separate all of these things.

I will attempt to make one thing crystal-clear: if you go for quality of life first, invariably your standard of living goes up, but if you just go for standard of living, there's no assurance that your quality of life is going to go up. We will deal with all of these.

The principle we're going to be teaching through this book is the principle that made our country great. Did you ever wonder why it is that in 1776, 3 million Americans produced Washington and Hamilton and Jefferson and Madison and Monroe and Franklin, and why it is in 1995, 265 million Americans produced—I'll let you fill in the blanks?

I don't believe you can name one person with the stature of the individuals I have just named. Let me ask you. Could it be what they were taught? As you reflect on it, do you believe that what you teach has anything to do with what you believe, and what you believe has anything to do with what you do, and what you do has anything to do with what you have?

Let me tell you what they were taught. According to the Thomas Jefferson Research Institute, in the 1770s, over 90 percent of all of the education had a moral, ethical, faith basis—solid foundation stuff. That's the reason we produced all of the people we did in that period of our history.

So many times people think, "Well, I'm just an accountant or a bookkeeper or a salesperson or a household executive or a doctor or a lawyer or whatever. What can I do?"

Again—yes, you were designed for accomplishment. You're engineered for success. You're endowed with the seeds of greatness. You're fearfully and wonderfully made. You were born to win, but it takes a plan.

When I was writing my book *Over the Top*, my daughter was the editor. She's the best editor, by far, I have ever had. We completed a manuscript. We sent it to the publisher, and he promptly packed it up and sent it back and said, "How can you tell people how to go over the top when you haven't identified what the top is?"

I thought to myself, "Well, that's a big snap." I worked for two solid months. I would write, and no, that's not it. I'd write some more. No, that's not it. I'd try again. I'd get out and take those long walks and nothing was happening. I didn't have a clue.

Then one day the redhead and I were in Shreveport, Louisiana. We were there visiting her sister, who's in a nursing home. She has MS. Many of the people in that home are beyond human help.

I'm a solution-oriented guy. Somebody says, "Here's a problem." I say, "Step number one is this, step number two is this, step number three is that." But some of those people unfortunately are beyond this kind of human help.

The redhead is not burdened with the belief that she has to solve people's problems. She just walks in, grabs them, and starts hugging them and starts telling them how pretty they are, how much she loves them, how glad she is to see them, and they gather around her like bees at a hive.

On that particular day, I couldn't handle it. I walked out. As I walked out, I was praying. I said, "Lord, give me that kind of heart. Make me have that kind of compassion for my fellow human being. Touch me so that I will have that kind of spirit."

In a few minutes, I felt better. I walked back in. They were in the big meeting room. My wife and her sister were seated at the table. I walked in and sat down, and all of a sudden, it started to come.

The only piece of paper I had was the back of the motel bill, which I had just paid. I took the bill out, and I started writing. Ninety percent of this is what I wrote in those few minutes after I'd struggled for two months.

You're at the top when you clearly understand that failure is an event, not a person, that yesterday ended last night, and today is your brand-new day. You've made friends with your past or focused on the present, and you are optimistic about your future. You're at the top when you know that success, a win, doesn't make you, and failure, a loss, doesn't break you, when you're filled with faith, hope, and love, and live without anger, greed, guilt, envy, or thoughts of revenge.

You're at the top when you're mature enough to delay gratification and shift your focus from your rights to your responsibilities. You're at the top when you know that the failure to stand for what is morally right is the prelude to being the victim of what is criminally wrong.

You're at the top when you're secure in who you are so you are at peace with God and in fellowship with man. You're at the top when you've made friends of your adversaries and have gained the love and respect of those who know you best, and when you understand that others can give you pleasure, but genuine happiness comes when you do things for others.

You're at the top when you're pleasant to the grouch, courteous to the rude, and generous to the needy. You're at the top when you've loved the unlovable, given hope to the hopeless, friendship to the friendless, and encouragement to the discouraged.

You're at the top when you can look back in forgiveness, forward in hope, down in compassion, and up with gratitude. You're at the top when you know that he who would be the greatest among you must become the servant of all.

You're at the top when you recognize, confess, develop, and use your God-given physical, mental, and spiritual abilities to the glory of God and for the benefit of mankind. You're at the top when you stand in front of the Creator of the universe, and he says to you, "Well done, thou good and faithful servant."

After I identified the top, I realized what I'd really done. I'd identified the bottom. That's the base. That's the foundation upon which you can build any kind of career, whether it's in education, athletics, business, medicine, law, accounting, computers, or whatever. I believe these are principles that will make a difference.

What happens to people when they have no hope? I have a good friend. Her name is Pam Lontos. Pam was an overweight, depressed housewife. For five years she had been under the care of a psychiatrist who assured her every time they got together that she would always need him because she was never going to get any better; he was her only hope.

She was sleeping from twelve to eighteen hours every day. She only got up to prepare breakfast for her children and husband, and then she went back to bed. She got up again to prepare them dinner, and she went back to bed again. That was her daily routine, and it had been going on for several years.

Then one day she heard an advertisement on the radio. The advertisement was about a health club, and it piqued her interest. For the first time in a long time, she caught a glimmer of hope.

As a story within a story, General Robinson Risner is a friend of mine. He was a prisoner of war in the Hanoi Hilton for seven years. For five and a half years he was in solitary confinement in a minute cell. The way he kept from losing his mind was that he would jog in place by the hour, right there in his cell. Still, on occasion, it was so depressing in there that he would take his underwear and stuff it in his mouth and scream at the top of his voice. He did not want the enemy to know that they were getting to him.

One day in the depth of his despair, he was down on the floor in this little cinderblock cell, and he started crawling around and putting his eye up against the wall, hoping he could see something on the outside.

There was a minute crack, and he saw a single leaf, and he said, "You will never know what it meant to me to see a single, green leaf after having seen no sign of life other than my tormentors all of these years."

I don't know how that story impacts you, but when I heard that, I made a new resolution, and that was I'd be very careful about what I complained about and very sensitive to the things that I have to be grateful for.

Back to Pam Lontos. That day, she listened to the radio and caught just a glimpse of hope from what that commercial said. She decided to get up and go down to that health club. She saw lots of people there, and everybody was smiling, everybody was busy, everybody seemed to be in a good mood and having fun. She decided to join.

That's step number one, and that's so important. We all have to have that first step my friend Joe Sabba has said: you don't have to be great to start, but you have to start to be great.

Pam saw that. She had taken that first step. She joined the club, and when she started exercising, she started feeling so much better. As a matter of fact, she got a job selling the enrollments in that club and was very successful at it, but she was very spasmodic. She was up and down. She was on a roller-coaster, because you don't cure depression like that just by a few exercises and a few weeks.

Her manager gave her a set of my tapes. She started listening to those tapes, and that was an encouragement that she needed to fuel the hope. She stabilized her productivity, which consistently got better and better, and then she decided she wanted to sell radio advertising, because she really loved radio.

She applied at her favorite station. They weren't even interviewing anybody, wouldn't even talk to her. But if you have hope, you'll take action. She just showed up at 8:00, when the manager got there, and stood just outside of his office from 8:00 until 5:00, when he left. She did it one day, two days, three days, and on the fourth day the manager said, "You know, I believe this girl wants a job."

He interviewed her, and bottom line is she sold him. She got the job, and almost immediately she became the number-one salesperson there. A few months later, she was outproducing the other four salespeople combined. Then she got a big break. She broke her leg, and it was a serious break. She was in a cast from her hip to her ankle. The doctor said, "It's going to be ten months before you'll be able to go back to work."

Ten days later, she showed back up at the radio station on crutches, hobbling around. She hired a driver to drive her around, but it was so difficult getting in and out of cars, she knew she had to do something else. But now she'd been fed with hope. She'd seen what she was able to do. She'd seen the changes that came through the inevitable question: "What can I do now?" People with hope get to be creative, you see. "What can I do now that will enable me to remain or retain my productivity? I simply cannot fight this getting in and out of the car a dozen times a day, and sometimes the person I want to see is not even there." She started studying telephone selling and became so good at it that her productivity went up.

Then the other salespeople came to her and said, "Tell us what you're doing." She started teaching them. Then the sales manager quit, and they petitioned management to make Pam the sales manager, and they did. Now she really got busy, and production doubled and tripled. As a matter of fact, it was with the Disney Radio chain, so they started taking her to other radio stations, and productivity went up in every case.

She was invited to speak, and after a few weeks, they made her the vice-president in charge of sales. Here's a lady who, three and a half years earlier, had a psychiatrist tell her she was never going to do anything because she was going to be depressed all her life, and now she's the vice-president in charge of sales for Disney Radio.

They invited her to speak at the National Radio Broadcasters Association, and she was so effective that eighteen stations invited her to come do some training in their company. Today she's a published author and an internationally known speaker. She started with hope.

I want to read something written by Dr. Joseph Sizu, and the title of it is "Unsung Heroes."

Let it never be forgotten that glamor is not greatness. Applause is not fame. Prominence is not eminence. The man of the hour is not apt to be the man of the ages. A stone may sparkle, but that does not make it a diamond. A man may have money, but that does not make him a success. It is what the unimportant do that really counts and determines the course of history. The greatest forces in the universe are never spectacular. Summer showers are more effective than hurricanes, but they get no publicity. The world would soon die but for the fidelity, loyalty, and consecration of those whose names are unhonored and unsung.

What else do you have to look at? Let me ask you this: do you have a racehorse worth over a million dollars?

If you did have one, let me ask you a question: Would you keep him up half the night, letting him drink coffee and booze and smoke cigarettes and eat junk food? If you did, how many races would he win? I think you'd probably agree he wouldn't win very many races. Would you treat a ten-dollar dog that way? A five-dollar cat?

What about a billion-dollar body? "Oh, but that's mine. I'm doing it to *me*." Well, what do you have against *you*?

You have to look at all aspects: the physical, the mental, and the spiritual. In the last twenty-three years, I've read an average of three hours a day. I read a little bit of everything. I try to read my Bible every day and the daily newspaper every day. That way I know what both sides are up to.

We need to get balanced information. You have to look at the spiritual side of life, among other things. You're going to be dead lots longer than you're going to be alive.

The April 28, 1986 issue of *Fortune* magazine talked about a study they did of the CEOs of the Fortune 500 companies. Over 50 percent of them came from lower-middle-class or poor families; 91 percent of them were either Catholic, Jewish, or Protestant. There was evidence that they were at least semi-active in their faith, meaning they got their ethics, their morals, their judgment, their values, their wisdom out of the Bible.

Have you ever wondered why 65 percent of college graduates, 72 percent of Rhodes Scholars, 75 percent of military-academy graduates, 65 percent of U.S. congressmen, 85 percent of airline pilots, 85 percent of FBI agents, and eleven out of twelve astronauts who walked on the moon were all Boy Scouts, according to the autumn 1992 issue of *The American Scholar*?

Let me see if I can explain why. First of all, Boy Scouts talk to themselves. I'm going to do a lot of talking about self-talking, because that is one of the keys to success.

All of us talk to ourselves. As a matter of fact, you talked to yourself on the way down here tonight: "I wonder if they're going to get started before we get there. Will there be a seat for me? Where should I park my car? I hope Sally's going to be here." We do it all the time.

Every Thursday night in Yazoo City, Mississippi, I used to stand up there as a Boy Scout and say, "On my honor"—boy, isn't that a great word?—"I will do my best to do my duty to God and my country, to obey the Scout Law, to help other people at all times, to keep myself physically strong, mentally awake, and morally straight."

Boy, that is good stuff. And the Scout Law says a Scout is trustworthy, loyal, helpful, friendly, courteous, kind, obedient, cheerful, thrifty, brave, clean, and reverent. If you were an employer, how many of you would like to have all of your employees with all these qualities? Would an individual like that have a pretty good chance of having a little more job security?

Let me tell you something else the Scouts did. One Thursday night a month, we had Court of Honor. That's when we stood up there, and we were given the merit badges for what we had been doing.

We knew exactly what it took to be a first-class Scout. We had the merit badges all laid out. That's goal setting. We knew what it took to be an Eagle Scout, and Eagle Scouts are successful in all facets of life to an extent that goes far beyond their numbers.

If I was raising a young boy or a young girl today, I'd have them in the Boy Scouts, the Cub Scouts, the Girl Scouts. You know their mantra is "Be prepared," and you know what they say: do a good deed every day. Understand that you can have everything in life you want if you will just help enough other people get what they want.

The Scouts teach leadership. I was talking with Scout executives just this week, and they explained to me at the first camp they have somebody teaching the young Scout how to drive the stakes and set the tent up. At the next Scout camp, the kid who was learning is now teaching. That's the way you learn things. You hear, you forget. You see, you remember. If you see it and hear it and do it, you understand, and you're successful at it.

To go back to self-talk: the most important opinion you have is the opinion you have of yourself, and the most important conversation you will have today is the conversation that you will have with yourself.

Recently a study validated that what you say to yourself has a direct bearing on your performance. Dr. Joyce Brothers says you cannot consistently perform in a manner which is inconsistent with the way you see yourself.

A lot of people say, "I don't talk to myself," but interestingly, the same person talks to the driver of another car three blocks away—with considerable feeling, I hasten to add. You're not going to believe this, but some people even talk to golf balls: "Go in the hole, stay in there." You know exactly what I'm talking about.

So we're going to have you talking to yourself, and that's going to be fun. Now we're going to have some fun too. There was a lady in Dallas, sixty-five years old, who watched an exercise video. She got all motivated. She went home and told everybody, "I'm going to start an exercise program. I'm going to start walking. I'm going to walk five miles a day every day for the rest of my life, starting today."

Her family tried to talk her out of it. They said, "That's too much. You don't start with five miles. Start with one mile."

"No, I'm going to walk five miles a day every day for the rest of my life."

She is now eighty-three years old, and her family doesn't have a clue as to where she is.

We're going to be talking about change. Change is stressful, but so are unemployment and bankruptcy. One statement from Alcoholics Anonymous says that one definition of insanity is to think you can keep on doing the same thing and somehow get different results. The truth is if you keep on doing what you've been doing, you're going to keep on getting what you've been getting. If you like what you've been getting, that's fine, but if you don't like what you're getting, then, ladies and gentlemen, maybe we need to explore some changes.

I want to have you thinking big. Let me share with you our mission statement at the Zig Ziglar Corporation. It is to be the difference maker in the personal, family, and business lives of enough people to make a positive difference in America and the world.

I know that's pretentious. We're a small company, but let me tell you why our mission is not impossible. Let me share with you why it is possible.

I love this story of the grandfather walking on the beach with his grandson. Every step or two, the grandfather would reach down, pick up a sand dollar, and throw it out to sea. He'd take a couple of more steps, pick up another one, and throw it out. Finally the grandson said, "Granddaddy, what are you doing?"

The grandfather said, "Son, these sand dollars are living organisms. If I don't throw them out to sea, they'll die in the hot sun. They've been washed ashore by the tide."

"But, Granddaddy, they are thousands of them. What possible difference can it make?"

The grandfather reached down, picked up another one, threw it out to sea, and said, "To this one, it makes all the difference in the world."

We're going to be talking about significant things. We're going to explore why immigrants—I'm talking about legal immigrants, whether they're from the Orient or South America or Africa or the Middle East—are four times as likely to become millionaires in America as are the people who are born here.

It was explained to me in minute detail by a little four-year-old girl. Three or four years ago, I got aboard an aircraft in Dallas headed for Norfolk, Virginia. I was the first passenger aboard. I was seated in seat 2C. A mother and her three little ones got aboard right behind me. She was carrying the infant, leading the toddler. The four-year-old was following behind.

The little four-year-old got on board, and she looked left into the cockpit and saw those three impressive figures with all the boards, and she saw the electronic gadgets there, probably more than she had ever seen in her lifetime. When she turned around, those little eyes were as big as the proverbial saucers.

I don't know why, but the child put her little hands on her little legs just above her knees. She bent down, and she looked down that long fuselage and said it all with one word, "Gosh."

Gosh. That's what immigrants say when they get to America. They've left it all behind them, friends and family and support groups, climate and culture and language. They come into this land without the things that so many have. The first thing they do when they land in America is get the daily paper. They look up the jobs that are available. They would pick up the Dallas paper and say, "There's 291 jobs advertised today, some of them paying over $5 an hour. Where I come from, that's three days' wages. I'll work not just eight hours a day, I'll work twelve hours. I'll get my education at a community college. I will live cheaply. I will save my money. I will take advantage of the opportunities that are here," and by the time they find out we have problems, it's too late. They've already made it.

In 1990 the number-one selling T-shirt in Japan was "We're number one." The number-one selling T-shirt in America was "Underachiever and proud of it."

Too many people born in America get up every morning and say, "Big deal." The immigrant gets up and says, "Wow, what a deal." What a difference it makes. We're going to be looking at why that is so important. They come here with a vision, with a mission. A vision is a clearly articulated, results-oriented picture of a future you intend to create.

I'll not tell you this is easy. It's not. I believe—and know, as a matter of fact—that life is tough, but I also know that when you're tough on yourself, life is going to be infinitely easier on you.

Here's what they have on the wall in a church in Sussex, England: "A vision without a task is but a dream. A task without a vision is drudgery, but a vision and a task are the hope of the world." I believe that is absolutely true—not easy, but it's worth it.

All of my life, I have thought I was an optimist, until I heard about this lady who moved into a retirement home. On the very first day at lunch, she was seated across the table from a gentleman who was there. After a moment or two, he became concerned about the fact that she was really eyeballing him. I mean, she was staring a hole through him.

He grew uncomfortable, and finally he said, "Ma'am, I don't understand. Why are you staring at me?" She said, "I can't believe it." He said, "You can't believe what?" She said, "I can't believe that you look exactly like my third husband—the color of your eyes, your mannerisms, the way you talk, your age, your size. You look exactly like my third husband."

He said, "Third husband? How many times have you been married?"

She said, "Twice."

I want you to know that people can change. I want you to know even animals can change. This past week the redhead and I were down at our home at Holly Lake, Sugarville. We were out walking our little dog. We have a little Welsh Corgi, and his name is Taffy.

We were out walking, and we met this other couple, and they had a little dog, except he was about three times as big as our little dog. He was a beautiful dog—healthy-looking, gorgeous fur, the whole bit. We got to talking, as dog owners always do. I said, "That's such a beautiful dog. It looks so healthy. What are you feeding that dog?"

"Turnip greens," the man said.

"I never heard of anyone feeding a dog turnip greens. My dog wouldn't eat turnip greens."

He said, "Mine wouldn't either for the first three weeks."

Too many times, we forget that we are measured by far more than just our intellect. For example, Mike Singletary played linebacker for the Chicago Bears. He was All-Pro. He was drafted as late as he was because his time in the forty-yard dash was not really that good. Not only that, but he was too short. What they could not measure, though, was just how badly he wanted to be the best at what he was doing.

Nor did they know that there was a shorter distance that for linebackers was even more important. That's the way you got off the ball, and so when he was playing linebacker there for the Chicago Bears, when a running back would break through the line of scrimmage, the typical linebacker would cut him off about seven or eight yards down the field. Singletary started so fast that many times he caught them *at* the line of scrimmage. He held them to two-yard gains where the others were permitting five-, six-, seven-, and eight-yard gains. They couldn't measure that.

Emmitt Smith—same story. You know, he's not really fast on the forty-yard dash. We see him run down from behind from time to time, but off the ball, at that first accelerated moment, he is really fast. That's the reason he can get through that hole and pick up that yardage time after time.

Jerry Rice—same story. All three of these players were drafted later than they would have been because they were just timing the forty-yard dash. What they had not determined at that point was an unusual characteristic Jerry Rice had, and that is when he was running stride-by-stride with a defender, and he looked up and saw the ball in the air, he had another gear reserved especially for that occasion, and though they'd been running neck-and-neck, all of a sudden he put it in that other gear, and he just pulled off and left the guy.

Some things you just can't measure. This is what I really want to talk about to you. See, all three of these men had tremendous pride in what they did. Bible students occasionally say that pride is kind of a dirty word. Let me tell you something about words. They change meaning.

For example, if I were to look at you and say, "You're silly," you'd be offended unless you knew that the word *silly* comes from *saelig*, an Old English word that means *blessed, happy, healthy,* and *prosperous*. So if anybody ever calls you silly again, you ought to just grin and say, "Man, you don't know how right you are. You got it right on the button."

What does this have to do with pride? The Bible is talking about false pride, or vanity. Pride is an honest evaluation of that which is good. Could it possibly be wrong for me to say to my children, "I am proud of the values you have?" Could it be wrong for me to say to my staff, "I am so proud of the job that you do"?

I love the acrostic *pride* forms. It is Personal Responsibility in Daily Endeavors. Pride is important. For the first fifteen years of my career, I was in direct sales. I've knocked on tens of thousands of doors in my lifetime. I don't ever remember getting excited about going out and knocking on doors. I did it because that's one of the things I had to do to make sales.

After a period of time, I started putting on cooking demonstrations, where the hostess would invite in several couples, and we'd cook up the meal and make the sales. I finally got semismart and realized I couldn't do it all myself. I ran an ad in Columbus, South Carolina, for a lady to help me. A lady named Jerry Arrowwood responded.

To give you an idea of what her personality was like, she was baking cakes and taking in sewing to help support her three daughters. Does that tell you something about her? Very quiet, very shy, but also very neat. I told her that in essence I wanted her to do the cooking, wash the dishes, clean the cookware, and clean the kitchen. A real top-level job.

She said, "Oh, Zig, I'd love to have that job. I love to cook, don't mind washing dishes, don't even mind cleaning the kitchen, but as you can tell, I'm very shy. I have to get a promise from you that you will never call on me to participate in the actual demonstration itself. In other words, Zig," she said, "you do the talking, I'll do the working."

I could instantly tell that Jerry and I were going to get along real good—no conflict of interest there. Well, we did for a couple of months, and then one night my mouth overloaded my back. I made too many promises. I said, "Jeri, you have to help me."

"What do you want me to do?"

"I want you to deliver these six sets of cookware I've sold and teach the husband and wife how to use them on their own stove."

Sheer terror filled her eyes. She physically started shaking instantly. "I can't do it. I can't do it."

"You can't do *what*, Jeri?"

"I can't deliver that cookware and teach those people how to use it on their stoves."

"Jeri, I said, "every night for the last two months, that's what you've been doing to the host and hostess."

"Yes, but you're always here, and if I foul up, I know you'll bail me out."

"Jeri, it's not that big a deal." I didn't even come close to making that sale. She just wasn't buying any of it. We had a twenty-five- or thirty-mile drive back home. It was very quiet. She was obviously thinking about it.

Then, just as she started to get out of the car, she turned to me and said, "All right. I'll do it. I'm not going to sleep a wink tonight. I'll probably foul up the deal tomorrow, but you stuck your neck out, you got the people's money, you told them it'd be delivered tomorrow. I don't want to hurt your reputation, so I'll do it. But, I'm going to tell you something, Zig. If you ever do this again," she said, "it's going to be your neck. It ain't going to be mine. I'm not going to ever do this again."

She got out of the car, and I don't know if she slept that night or not. I know I didn't. The next night, I got one of the most exciting telephone calls I have ever gotten in my life. It came in about 9:00. It took me about forty minutes to get that introvert off the telephone. I mean, she word-by-word, step-by-step, blow-by-blow gave me in minute detail everything that took place.

She said, "When I got to the first family, Zig, they had the coffee made and a dessert on, and we had a wonderful time. They told me how personable I was, what a great personality I had, how professional I was. Zig," she said, "I had a wonderful time there, and three of the six couples had the coffee on and the dessert ready, and they all bragged on me. Zig, I'm telling you I had the time of my life. I'll do this any time you want to do it."

Didn't happen that year or the next or the next or the next, but a little less than five years later, Jerry Arrowwood was the vice-president in charge of sales training internationally for a multimillion-dollar cosmetic company.

You know what I believe? I believe with all of my heart there will be tens of thousands of Jerry Arrow-woods who will hear this, and they will reason—accurately—that "if she can do it, I can do it too."

I have one major regret in this whole episode, and that is I did not retain the name and address of the first couple that she delivered that set of cookware to. She approached that first home with fear and trembling. She was in a mad dash. She couldn't wait to get to the second one.

It's amazing what a word of encouragement will do. Somebody once said that a lot of people have gone a lot further than they thought they could because somebody else thought they could. That first couple had a profound impact. They're unsung heroes. They really did something for Jerry Arrowwood.

Have you ever noticed that normally when somebody says, "I'm going to tell you something for your own good," they tell you something bad? Did it ever occur to us that if we're going to tell somebody something for their own good, we ought to tell them something *good* for their own good?

This is an old principle. A hundred years ago, Andrew Carnegie had forty-three millionaires working for him—and a hundred years ago, a millionaire was a rich dude. A reporter got wind of it and asked him, "Mr. Carnegie, how on earth did you hire forty-three millionaires?" Mr. Carnegie said, "None of them were millionaires when I hired them."

"Then what did you do to develop them to the degree that they became so valuable to you that you could pay them so much money they became millionaires?"

Carnegie taught us a great lesson when he said, "You develop people in the same way you mine gold. When you go in a gold mine, you expect to move tons of dirt to get an ounce of gold, but you don't go in there looking for the dirt. You go in there looking for the gold."

I believe there's a gold mine inside of everybody we deal with. I believe that people have a great deal more inside of them than they realize. It took an awful lot of courage for Jerry Arrowwood to take that first step. Courage is not the absence of fear. It's going ahead despite the fear.

Shakespeare said, "The applause of a single human being is of great consequence." When Jerry got that first round of applause, she liked it so much she started doing other things. She became a student. She started learning. She became excited about growing in life, and when people are growing, then they are generally excited. When you're learning things, that's what creates excitement.

Jerry was a very humble person. Humility is one of the great qualities of leadership. When a person is humble, it doesn't mean that they think less of themselves. It simply means they think of themselves less. Over a period of time, Jerry's confidence grew, but it never turned to arrogance.

When you get arrogant, that's when Buster Douglas knocks out Mike Tyson. For the benefit of those of you who are not fight fans, that's when Mike was the unbeatable heavyweight champion of the world and Buster Douglas was almost a nobody. They weren't even betting on it because Mike was such a prohibitive favorite, and that was the last fight Buster Douglas ever won.

Jerry Arrowwood retained her humility. She built her confidence. She worked very, very hard. She became a student, but she took what she had and developed it. That's one of the reasons I will say so many times to you that you need to listen to your tapes over and over. You see, they keep hope alive. When you hear these things going in your mind over and over, you're going to get a lift. Throughout this book, I will say, I bet, fifty times that you can have everything in life you want if you will just help enough other people get what they want.

I'm certain that when Jerry Arrowwood got out of the car that night to deliver that cookware, she wasn't thinking, "Zig's been telling me I can everything in life I want if I just help enough other people get what they want, and what I want to be is vice-president in charge of sales training for that big, old cosmetics company. And if I deliver these cookware sets, then I'll get to be the vice-president"—now isn't that insane?

She did it because it was the right thing to do. I was in a jam. She felt loyalty to me and a concern for me as a friend and as her employer. I'm not talking about a tactic. I'm talking about a philosophy.

CHAPTER 3

The Day before Vacation

Let me ask you a question. As a rule, do you get more work done on the day before you go on vacation than you normally get done in two, three, even four ordinary days?

Now if you can figure out why and how and repeat it every day without working any harder, does it make sense that you'd be more valuable to yourself, your company, your family, and your community? The answer is yes, it does make a whole lot of sense.

I want to make another profound statement: what you do *off* the job determines how far you go *on* the job.

Every athlete knows that. Every entertainer knows that. Every public speaker ought to know that. If every other worker doing anything would learn that, they would be getting ahead much faster in life.

They did a study of the typical American manufacturing plant. The person working the line on an hourly basis watched an average of thirty hours of television a week. The person in charge of that line watched an average of twenty-five hours of television a week. The foreman watched an average of twenty hours of television a week. Are you noticing a little trend here?

The plan superintendent watched an average of fifteen hours of television a week. The vice-president of the plant watched an average of twelve to fifteen hours of television a week. The president watched an average of eight to twelve hours of television a week. The chairman of the board watched an average of four to eight hours of television a week, and for 50 percent of that time, they were watching training videos.

What do you think would happen to that person who's watching thirty hours of television a week if they were to take ten of those hours and get involved in what you're doing right now: reading good books, listening to tapes, attending valuable seminars, getting that education? Are they a victim of circumstances, or is it because they're a victim of inertia?

The biggest damage television does is what it keeps you from doing. It keeps you from talking to folks, it keeps you from exercising, it keeps you from reading, it keeps you from learning, it keeps you from associating with other people, developing friendships, and 101 other things.

What all this leads up to is this: on the night before the day before vacation, did you get out a little sheet of paper and say to yourself, "Now, self, tomorrow you have to do this and this and this"?

In its simplest form, that is goal setting. I do a lot of public seminars where I'm fortunate enough to be on the program with some real celebrities in life. I mean, President Ford, President Bush, Schwarzkopf, Colin Powell. Is that OK for name dropping? Don't misunderstand. I don't classify them as buddies. I'd love to. I am proud of the fact that the last time I saw Colin Powell, he did give me a big, old hug, and since he's one of my heroes, I kind of liked that.

Anyhow, I do a lot of those public seminars. Now, they did a study, and who is *they*? *They* is David Jensen, the chief administrative officer for the Crump Institute of Molecular Imaging in the department of pharmacology in the UCLA School of Medicine.

He did a study on the people who came to the seminars. It represents a broad section of American industry, everybody from psychiatrists and truck drivers to schoolteachers and household executives, salespeople, entrepreneurs, business owners, all kinds of people. Those who set goals and developed a plan of action to get there earned an average of $7,401 a month. Those who did not set goals earned an average of $3,397 a month. That's over $4,000 a month difference.

As you read this, I want you to answer the question for yourself. Do you have time to invest another ten minutes a day to pick up another $4,000 a month?

Here's the rest of the story. The survey also showed that these people not only earned the additional money, but were happier and healthier and got along better with the folks at home. People who know where they're going, and have a plan to get there, are easier to get along with. That's what this boils down to.

You set those goals, and then you have to organize. In other words, you say, "First of all, I'm going to do this," and you lay it out. You kind of see your hand. Now you get organized. Once you have it organized, you accept the responsibility. You say, "This is what I am going to do." You accept the responsibility. That's something a lot of us don't like to do, and it goes back to Adam and Eve.

You remember the story. They were in the Garden of Eden. God gave it all to them. He said, "You can have everything you want, but there's a tree right in the middle of the garden. Leave it alone. Don't eat from it." You know what happened. They ate the fruit. A lot of people say it was the apple in the tree that caused man's problems. Not so. It was the pair on the ground that created the problem.

You know what happened. God came walking in the garden that evening and said, "Adam, where are you?" Now God knew where Adam was, but he wanted Adam to say, "Over here, Lord."

"Adam, did you eat that fruit?" God knew the answer, but he wanted Adam to fess up, but Adam did the manly thing and has passed it on to every generation since. He said, "Lord, let me tell you about that woman."

The Lord said, "Eve, did you eat that fruit?"

She kept the ball rolling. She said, "Lord, let me tell you about that snake." Of course, the snake didn't have a leg to stand on.

Now I know that theologically I don't have a leg to stand on with that last statement either, but here's the point. You don't have a leg to stand on, I don't have a leg to stand on, when we constantly blame other people in the past. Realistically, if somebody fouled up your past, you're not going to give them permission to ruin your future, are you?

We have to get serious about doing something about our future. We have to get serious about doing things with our lives. Now let me go ahead and say something you might already have noticed.

I speak and write at the seventh-grade level. I do it deliberately, because I learned a few years ago that if you keep it there, even the college professors will be able to follow along with you.

See, college professors are people. My good friend, Dr. Steve Franklin, a college professor at Emory University, says, "You know, Zig, the great truths in life are simple. You don't need three moving parts and four syllables for it to be significant. Think about it for a moment, Zig. There are only three pure colors on the face of this earth, but look at what Michelangelo did with those colors. There are only ten mathematical digits, but look at what Einstein did with them. There are only seven notes, but look what Chopin and Beethoven and Vivaldi did with those seven notes. Look at what Elvis did with two."

Lincoln's Gettysburg Address is 262 words, and 202 of them are one syllable. Simple, direct. John 3:16: twenty-five words, twenty-one of them one syllable. I believe in keeping it simple. I believe in making it so plain that nobody can miss what is being said.

Now you've gotten organized, and you've accepted the responsibility, and you've made the commitment. Most people are about as committed as a kamikaze pilot on his thirty-ninth mission. They just don't take it seriously.

I well remember January 7, 1992. I rode past the Plano, Texas, Recreation Center. That's where I do my exercises and weight lifting. (Had to stop the weight lifting. I was bulking up, and a lot of folks thought I was on steroids, and we can't have that.)

I rode past the center, because there was not a parking space. I was back over there the next day, and this time I squeezed in, but in the Nautilus room, they had lines behind every machine—three, four, five, or six deep. You can't exercise three minutes and rest for fifteen, so I went back outside to the desk and asked the young man, "Sean, what on earth's going on?

Sean laughed and said, "Oh, Zig don't give it a thought. Give us about three weeks. This will be back to normal. These are our New Year's resolution people."

You see, a New Year's resolution is really nothing but a New Year's confession. "I confess I have to lose some weight. I confess I have to get better organized. I confess I have to get more education. I confess I have to spend more time with my family. I confess I have to quit smoking." The confession lasts as long as it's convenient, requires no trouble, takes no time, and involves no pain.

Now that I've said that, let me say that confession is extraordinarily important, because it can be step one, and you have to have step one before you can take step two.

This is where it gets to be important. If you tell enough people, "I'm going to quit smoking, I'm going to get an education, I'm going to get better organized," and you repeat it enough times, one day, all of a sudden, it finally breaks through.

A message can go 24,000 miles around the world in less than a tenth of a second, but sometimes it takes years for it to get that last one-sixteenth of an inch.

One day, though, it finally gets through. You confess it enough times, and then you verbally stomp your foot and say, "I'm going to do it." You've made a decision, and the way the mind works is really very simple. Once you've made a decision, then you say to yourself, "Now, self, if you're going to do that, you're going to have to get yourself a plan of action."

Whether you build a house, want to build a better marriage, get a better education, lose thirty-seven pounds, whatever it is, if you have made a decision, start with the confession, move to a decision, and then you automatically say, "Hey, I have to get a plan of action."

Once you have a logical plan of action that you believe in, then you say, "I can do it." Now you've made the commitment. Why is commitment so important regardless of what area of life you're in? If you've made a commitment, whether it's to get the education, maintain the marriage, lose the weight, or whatever, when you hit the wall—not *if*, but *when*— the first thing you think about is "How can I solve the problem?" If you haven't made the commitment, you think, "How can I get out of this deal? See, we find what we are looking for.

Now on the way to work the next morning, you're talking to yourself like crazy: "The first thing I'm going to do when I get there is this. I know I can handle this, and I know I can do that. Yes, I'll take care of that."

When you get there, there's only one change you should make. Instead of the most important thing for number one, you ought to put the most disagreeable thing first. If you have to go deal with Charlie, if that sucker's been a thorn in your side, and you have to handle the situation today, you go deal with Charlie. But if he's number five on the list, you've finished number one, and you're thinking about Charlie. You finish number two, you have to deal with Charlie. Finish number three, you have to deal with Charlie. So get Charlie out of the way.

Like this old boy down home says, "Friend, if you're going to have to swallow a frog, you just don't want to look at that sucker too long. He ain't going to get no prettier. He really is not."

So you get there on time, maybe even a little earlier. (The boss likes that.) You don't look around and say, "I wonder what I ought to do first." You have a plan of action. You're a self-starter, and you are optimistic that you're going to be able to get the job done. You become the kind of person that would take their last $2 and buy a money belt. (I tell folks I'm so optimistic, I'll put a dime in the parking meter while the redhead goes shopping. If that's not optimism, I don't know what optimism is.)

OK, now you get started. You get your job done, and that start is so important. Joe Sabba put it this way: "You don't have to be great to start, but you have to start to be great." A lot of people never get started.

You're extremely enthusiastic. You just get carried away with it. Let me talk about enthusiasm a minute. Enthusiasm is kind of like running in the dark. You might get there, but you might get killed on the way. If you're going in the wrong direction, blind enthusiasm just means you're going to get to the wrong place quicker.

What you have here, though, is a plan of action. Enthusiasm with a plan of action will produce dramatic results. You're going on a lighted path. You decisively move from one thing to another. You focus on the issue at hand. You discipline yourself to stay with the task until that task is completed.

If somebody comes along and says, "Hey, did you watch that game last night?" you say, "I'd like to talk about that, but I have some things to do."

Have you noticed that as a rule, people with nothing to do want to do it with you? When you are organized and disciplined, moving from one take to another, somehow those people just don't get in the way. They see that you have something to do, and your enthusiasm and discipline show up, kind of like Little Johnny.

He was one enthusiastic kid. Second grader. One Friday afternoon, the teacher said, "Class, if anybody has any unusual experiences this weekend, let me know on Monday. The class will want to hear about it." On Monday morning, Little Johnny was a pistol. That kid was all over the place sitting still. The teacher could tell: "Johnny, I'll bet you had a good weekend."

"Yes, ma'am, I sure did."

"What did you do, Johnny?"

"Me and my daddy went fishing. We caught seventy-five catfish. They all weighed seventy-five pounds."

"Son, you know that's not the truth."

"Yes, ma'am, it is. My daddy's a great fisherman. I'm even better than he is. We caught seventy-five catfish. They all weighed seventy-five pounds."

"Now, Johnny, if I were to tell you that on the way to school this morning, just before I got here, a big, old 1,200-pound grizzly bear ran up out of nowhere and was just about to grab me and eat me up, when suddenly a little eight-pound yellow dog jumped up, grabbed him by the nose, threw him down, bounced him back and fourth, broke his neck, and killed him. Johnny, would you believe that?"

"Oh, yes, ma'am. As a matter of fact, that's my dog."

Enthusiasm is important. Discipline is important. Persistence is important. You see, 175 of the CEOs of the Fortune 500 companies are former U.S. Marines; twenty-six of our presidents served in the military. What do they teach in the military? They teach discipline and persistence and focus and organization and direction.

These are the qualities that will make you a better husband, a better wife, a better parent, a better employee, a better employer, the whole bit. Along that line, you know that positive mental attitude, that old PMA, kicks into gear.

I don't believe there's anybody in America that is as excited about positive mental attitude as I am. One reason is that I believe I understand what positive thinking will let you do. I also understand what positive thinking *won't* do. I get concerned when I hear some highly motivated, enthusiastic, gung-ho guy or gal get up and say, "Man, with positive thinking, you can do anything." That ain't positive thinking. That is New Age thinking.

Positive thinking will let you use the ability you have, and that is awesome. There are some things it won't let you do. For example, Shaquille O'Neal—over 300 pounds of highly motivated, enthusiastic, revved up, raring to go basketball player. One of the most positive thinkers I've ever seen, but he would be a total failure as a jockey.

Nate Newton plays the line for the Dallas Cowboys, 340 pounds, give or take a hundred. Also outstanding, positive, optimistic, really a neat guy. He couldn't make it, though, in ballet. I don't care how positive he is. I'm positive, but I can't slam-dunk a basketball, and I've tried. Twice. If you need major surgery, I'm positive, but I don't recommend me.

Positive thinking won't let you do everything, but it will let you do everything better than negative thinking will. Let me tell you about positive thinking. When we walked in here earlier today, this room was pitch-black. They flipped some switches. It became lighted. Flipping switches didn't generate electricity. It released it. Had it not already been generated, we'd still be in a dark room.

The youngster that thinks he can go in to take a test and pass it with positive thinking, but hasn't studied—he's going to flunk that sucker. But if he has studied, the positive thinking will release the information, and he can put it on paper. We can document hundreds of cases where when kids changed their attitude, they were able to call up the information and make dramatically better grades in class and in any area of life.

The truth is you become a very, very positive individual because you have a plan of action and you become a team player. Team play is extremely important. Positive thinking and team play kind of go together.

I love the story coach Lou Holtz tells. Incidentally, Lou Holtz has been using our goal setting system every since he was at the University of Arkansas. His Notre Dame team follows it. He uses the system to help his team pass and graduate. That's their first goal. Then he uses it to blend them into the team.

One of Lou's favorite stories is about this fellow who was out in a rural area, and his car slid in a ditch. There was a farm close by, and he went to the farmer and said, "Can you help me? I don't have a jack." The old farmer said, "Well, I got an old mule, Dusty, but he's kind of hard of hearing and getting kind of old. I don't know he can or not, but I'd be willing to give it a try."

They got old Dusty. They took him out, and they hooked him up to the car. The old farmer got behind him and in a very loud voice said, "Pull, Billy, pull." Nothing. "Pull, Roscoe, pull." Nothing. "Pull, Charlie, Pull." Nothing. "Pull, Dusty, Pull." Old Dusty pulled that car right out of the ditch.

The fellow said, "I don't understand. You were calling on Billy, and you were calling on Roscoe and Charlie, and there wasn't but one mule there. What are you doing?" He said, "Well, like I said, Dusty's getting kind of old. He's hard of hearing and can't see very good. To tell you truth, he's gotten a little negative in his old age. If he thought he had to pull that car out by himself . . . but as long as he though he had a lot of help there, the team was with him, he figured he could do it, and out it came."

I make another important point: Until he called Dusty by name, Dusty didn't move. That's one key right there. The name of another person is very, very important.

A giant Belgian horse on its own can pull 8,000 pounds. Hook him up with another giant Belgian, and the team will pull 17,000 pounds. Send them off to school, and teach them to pull in harmony, the team will pull over 25,000 pounds.

Can you imagine what would happen if we could get every member of your family, every member of your company to pull together? It's awesome. I believe the day is going to come when we're going to have everybody in our company on the same page, pulling in the direction and with the same objectives. When that happens, we will absolutely explode. You can count on it. The same thing will happen in your own company.

Teamwork is so important. The Houston Rockets this year are again the world champions in basketball. Knowledgeable basketball people—and that does not include me—say there were at least four other teams that had much better personnel than the Houston Rockets did, but the Rockets functioned as a team, and they had a team leader whom they greatly respected in Hakeem Olajuwon. Again they won the world championship.

To go back to that day before vacation, the interesting thing is when the day was over, although you had gotten two or three times as much done as you normally get done, you were highly energetic. At the end of that day, man alive, you were jumping up and down and bouncing around, and you couldn't wait to get home. On the way home, again, you were talking to yourself. The energy level was enormously high. You didn't have a tired bone in your body.

You know when you're the most exhausted? When you've tried to fool the boss all day long, when you've had to make work and act like you're busy. Those are the days that you really are exhausted, but today you are so delighted that your competence and your creativity take a giant step forward. You're on a roll. That momentum builds; you're getting things done, and you feel so good about yourself. That self-image just blossoms.

When she was washing dishes and cleaning cookware, Jerry Arrowwood took pride in the way she could leave that kitchen so spotless, the way she could make that cookware shine, the way she washed those dishes and always left that lady's kitchen in much better shape than it was when she got there. That's what I'm talking about. When you sign your name with pride to what you've done, you'll be doing a better job.

Now I'm going to ask you a question. Have I said a word about working harder, or am I talking about working smarter? The answer is *smarter*.

If this works so well in organizing your job and your career, do you think there's a chance that if you planned your family time, your vacation time, your exercise time, your social time, you would get more of each of them done? What do you think?

I believe I work more hours than 99 percent of people. At 5:00 this morning I was working, 6:00 yesterday morning I was working, 5:00 the day before. Here is it 10:00, and I'm still at it. Yet I probably spent more time with my wife today than you did with your mate or your children. We spent an hour at breakfast. We spent nearly an hour at lunch. We spent forty-five minutes at dinner, and we had a lot of conversations in between. I also got in my forty-six-minute walk this morning. You have to plan things if they're going to happen. They're not accidentally going to come about. When you put it all together, you get many more things done.

I'm talking about running your day by the clock and your life with a vision. If you put it together in that way, then you can get so many more things done.

If you're an employer, let me ask you: would you fire any employee who came to work and performed every day like we're talking about here? Or would you say, "Hey, I want to make that man or that woman a lifetime deal"? "I want them to be with me forever. As a matter of fact, I have a little raise in mind for them. Who knows? Maybe even a promotion."

Now you might say, "But, Zig, suppose the same thing happens to me that happened to my buddy. He worked at this company twenty-three years, and then the boss's son got out of college and came home, and that young whippersnapper took his job. No fault of mine, but I lost it. What do I do now?"

Let me ask you: if you'd worked every day like you do the day before vacation, what kind of recommendation do you think you'd get? Would it be fabulous? What about your sales talk when you go to apply for a job and the person doing the interviewing asks what experience you've had?

What if you can look at that them and say, "I've had forty-one years' experience being absolutely honest. My tests all indicate that I'm a very intelligent human being. My goals are clearly defined. I'm a well-organized person. I accept responsibility for performance. I make commitments and keep those commitments. The résumé I gave you, my work record, shows it clearly. I am a very punctual person. I'm always there when I'm supposed to be. I get started when I get there."

Think of the sales talk you can give. When you get to the end, you say, "I know I have a great self-image, and I'm highly competent. I believe these are the qualities that your company needs. I believe this is the experience you need. I can start immediately, unless it would be better to wait until Monday morning. What would you prefer?"

You might say, "Zig, come on, man. Is that real?" It's as real as today and tomorrow, folks, because the world is always looking for somebody with these qualities.

Let me ask you another question: if your company goes belly-up, will you get another job because you *worked* for XYZ Company or because you *performed* for XYZ Company? Now whose responsibility is it to perform?

We're not victims. Yes, there are things that we can do to build employment security. There is no question about that. As we look at the list we've been talking about, how many of those qualities right there are positive qualities? Anybody?

OK, you think honesty and intelligence, goals, being organized, responsibility—you think all of those are positive qualities, am I right on that? How many of them are leadership qualities? How many of them do you have?

Let me tell you something interesting. We deny our talents and abilities because to acknowledge or to confess them would commit us to using them. Isn't that something!

Let's look at a couple of other thoughts. You're the only one that can use your ability. It's an awesome responsibility. Oliver Wendell Holmes said, "It's tragic in America that we waste our natural resources, but it's infinitely more tragic that so many people go to their grave with their music still in them." All of that talent, all of that ability.

I think of Vince Robert and Jerry Arrowwood, and I think of all of these other people for whom some-thing had to happen to bring it out and put it to work. You have to use that ability, or it goes to the grave with you. Tragically, when you deny your talents and abil-ities, you deny yourself, your family, your company, and your society the fruits of those abilities.

I'm going to ask you to do something right now. Since you've confessed that these all are qualities that you have, I'm going to ask you to stand up and claim them right now.

Stand up and say, "I"—call out your name—"am an honest, intelligent, goal-directed person. I am organized, responsible, and committed. I am punctual, a self-starter. I'm optimistic and enthusiastic. I'm highly motivated, decisive, and focused. I am disciplined and persistent and have a tremendous positive mental attitude. I'm a team player, energetic, competent, and I have a magnificent self-image."

You survived, did you not? In all the years I've been doing this, not once have we ever had a loss because someone did this.

Let's look at something else. Taking those qualities that we've discussed: do you believe that if you used them every day, you would be happier, healthier, more prosperous, more secure, have more friends, greater peace of mind, better family relationships, and more hope for the future? Then just take what you've got, use it, and then develop some more.

Let me also say that motivation is the key. There's a lot of confusion about what motivation is all about. You might ask me, "Is motivation permanent?" The answer is no, it's not. Neither is bathing. Does that mean I'm opposed to bathing? No. I'm very excited about taking a good shower. (I hope you are, too, especially if you use that new twenty-three-hour deodorant. The company that makes it figures everybody's entitled to some time to themselves. There's another one called Stereo. It doesn't kill the odor, but at least you can't tell where it's coming from.)

Motivation is extremely important. Motivation gets you going. Habit gets you there. Make motivation your habit, and you'll get there quicker, and you'll have more fun on the trip.

Let me show you this diagram:

It shows a series of squares. I want you to count those squares. Most people automatically say there are four, eight, sixteen. Then, almost immediately, they say, "Shucks, the whole thing is a square." That makes it seventeenth, but right here in the middle—the center four—there is another square, and so that brings it up to eighteen. If you keep counting, you'll see that there are thirty squares there.

I'm not trying to trick you, but I'm like a cross-eyed discus thrower. I don't set any records, but man, I keep the crowd alert.

How many squares did I add to the original figure? None. All I did was point out ones that were already there.

I have been leading up to something, and that is the question I'm going to ask now: how much more did you know about your job the day before you went on vacation than you did twenty-four hours earlier?

OK. Do you still agree that you get two or three times as much work done on that day than you normally get done on any other day?

There's a reason for it. It's called *motivation*. Motivation is the spark that lights the fire of knowledge. It fuels the engine of accomplishment. It maximizes and maintains momentum.

Now think with me for a moment. How great would it be to know that you have a sales meeting that you and I are holding every day of your life? When you go to work, we're conducting a sales meeting. What that means is you'll get to your job excited.

The minute you leave the house, you ought to be thinking about your job. The minute you leave your job, you ought to be thinking about your home. You ought to be preparing to get into work, and then preparing to get back into your life at home, because they all do go together.

They did a study on 1,139 CEOs of major companies, the average income $356,000. That's pretty good income. Their number-one priority was their family. Their number-one asset was their integrity. I've had people telling me for years, "You know, Zig, when I get a little down, I pop in one of your tapes, and man, it always gives me a lift."

As a rule, do you deliberately drive your automobile until it's completely out of gas and you're at the mercy of other motorists to take you to get a refill? When you see the needle moving close to empty, do you say, "I have to go get some gas"?

People say to me, "When I get down, I pop in one of your tapes." Is that smart, or should they pop in the tape before they get down? It's easier to stay up than it is to get up.

Chances are that, although you've been sitting there absorbing this material, at this moment you're more energized physiologically than you were when you sat down.

Dr. Forest Tennant is in my judgment the number-one drug authority in America. He was a consultant for the Justice Department, the NFL, Texaco, for any number of other organizations, NASCAR included. Dr. Forest Tennant is a friend of mine. He went to a seminar I conducted out in Anaheim, California, back in 1989. The seminar was from 6:30 until 10:30

in the evening. The participants had been in an afternoon seminar from 12:30 to 4:30.

Before I started at 6:30, Dr. Tennant took blood samples from five of the people. When I got through, he took blood samples from the same five. The endorphin level was up to 300 percent higher when I got through, after 10:30 at night, than it had been when I started.

Since then, Dr. Tennant has done a series of other experiments. He has discovered, for example, that when the brain is activated, and that's what's happening right now, the other neurotransmitters come in and flood the system—serotonin, dopamine, norepinephrine, and endorphins, and a lot of the other neurotransmitters. You are physiologically energized, not just psychologically.

This was written up in the May 1989 *Meetings and Conventions* magazine. Here's what he said: "There is a biochemical basis for why people feel good after these talks. Something in hearing about success gives us an emotional charge that releases those chemicals into the bloodstream, and that makes the body function better. While these effects last no more than a few hours, regular doses of motivation will lead to better health, happiness and achievement."

I do all of my recordings in front of live audiences and insert the humor because we want to get those endorphins and dopamine flowing. They energize you physiologically. Dr. Tennant says listening to tapes early in the morning will jump-start the flow of serotonin. Serotonin is the neurotransmitter that makes you feel good about yourself. It doesn't hit the system full force until about 10:00 in the morning.

Remember I've been saying that you can have everything in life you want if you'll just help enough other people get what they want? There's another way to jump-start the flow of serotonin: do something nice for someone else. It's amazing how good you feel about yourself when you do something really nice for somebody else. I'm talking about a procedure that works. I'm talking about a philosophy that's centered around others.

As I've already told you, I was raised down in Yazoo City, Mississippi. We lived next door to some rich folks during the Depression years, and I was over there for lunch one day, as I tried to be every day. Don't misunderstand. Even though there was the Depression going on, we certainly had plenty to eat at our house. I know we had plenty, because if I ever passed my plate, they'd always tell me, "I know you've had plenty." So I know we had plenty.

On this particular day, the cook brought the biscuits out, and the biscuits were not as thick as my wrist. I looked at them. I said, "Maude, what on earth happened to your biscuits?" She gave that big, old tummy laugh and said, "I'll tell you about those biscuits. They squatted to rise, but they just got cooked in the squat."

That's the plight of most people. They get cooked in the squat. They have half a mind to do it, or they're going to do it, but they never take that first step. That's why I'm really saying.

How many times have you ever seen somebody get excited about something but say, "When the kids get out of school, then I'll really get involved"? The kids get out of school, and they say, "I didn't realize it, but I have to take them even more places now than I did before the end of school. When the kids get back in school, I'll have more time."

The kids get back in school, and they say, "It's the first time in seventeen years that dear old Central High finally got a win in football, and you have to support the kids. Wait until the football season is over, and then I'll really get involved." Football season ends. They say, "Well, here it is Thanksgiving and Christmas and New Year, and people don't want to be bothered this time of year with all that stuff. Wait until after the holidays are over, then man, I'll be ready to go. Wait, wait, wait. I know exactly what you're thinking, but let me tell you the way it is. I like to get everything lined up. I prepare. I draw a plan of action. I get all ready, and then, man, I really get started. I'll pass all these other folks that got the jump on me now, but after the holidays, you just watch."

After the holidays they say, "You know, the weather. Have you ever seen weather like this? Wait until the weather settles down, and then, man, I'll really get busy." After that, they get good weather and say, "I haven't wet a hook or hit a golf ball in I don't know when, and you said it yourself: a fellow can't work all the time. You have to have some recreation. Wait until after that, and then, man, I'll really get busy." Then after they hit a few golf balls, wet the hook a few times, they say, "It's almost time for the kids to get out of school." That's where we came in.

People who wait for Aunt Matilda to move out or for John to get on the day shift, people who wait for the tax rate to change or for the new models to come out, people who wait for the new senator to take office or the new advertising campaign to start, people who wait on changes out there before they do anything in here, invariably end up getting cooked in the squat.

This information isn't worth a hill of beans until you put it into action. When you put it into action, that's when things happen. I promise you I've not given you any theories. This is valid information that has been tested and tried by tens of thousands of people, and it works in any language that you want to put it in.

That's what I'm talking about. I'm encouraging you to buy the ideas that we've been talking about. Take this to heart. Put it to work, and do it now, because if you do, I will see you not just at the top. I'm going to see you over the top.

CHAPTER 4

The Power of Words

Thank you, and God bless you for being here. Sometimes it is fun and exciting. A couple of you were talking as you were walking in, and I couldn't help but overhear one of you say to the other one, "Well, I can't tell you anymore. I've already told you more than I heard." It's like a couple of folks talking; one of them said, "I hate to spread gossip, but I don't know what else you can do with it." One fellow said to me, "I hate gossip, so I'm only going to tell you this once."

Incidentally, I read a study some time back that said every third person was either remarkably handsome or amazingly beautiful. I'd like to get you right now to turn directly to the person on your left and look them over real good. Now turn directly to the person on your right, and look them over real good. Now, since it obviously ain't either one of them, then guess who!

It's so neat to see so many beautiful ladies here this morning. Not only do women dress our audiences up so much, but women are just so much more practical than men. Like this lady down home. A bum came up to her in the street and said, "Ma'am, would you give me a dollar for a sandwich?" She said, "Not until I've seen the sandwich." That's being practical.

One lady said, "I didn't want to marry him for his money, but that was the only way I could get it." That really is being practical.

In December 1989, in the redhead and I walked into Prestonwood Shopping Center. That's her favorite center. That's where she made the All-Mall team for eight years in a row and last year made MVP as Most Valuable Purchaser. We walked into the little eyeglass place. I needed some glasses, and a very energetic, enthusiastic young man came up. He said, "May I help you?"

Well, I was grateful for help. I said to him, "Yes, I need some of those glare-proof glasses."

He said, "Oh, are you a photographer?"

"No, I never got involved in photography because of all of the negatives."

"Are you a producer?"

"No, I'm a speaker."

"What do you speak on?"

"Motivation, positive thinking, leadership. I do a lot of family seminars, courtship after marriage, raising positive kids in a negative world. I do a lot in sales training, goal setting, and that sort of thing."

He brightened and said, "Oh, kind of like Zig Ziglar."

"Well, sort of."

The redhead pointed her finger at me and said, "This *is* Zig Ziglar."

He was a very cool young man. He backed up a couple of feet, looked me over pretty good, and started shaking his head. He said, "Oh, no. I've seen videotapes of Zig Ziglar, and Zig Ziglar is always jumping up and down. This is not Zig Ziglar."

I said to the redhead, "You see there, sweetheart, I told you we weren't going to be able to fool this young man. He's probably looking for some forty- or fifty-year-old codger, and he sees us two youngsters walk in. He looks me over real good, and he knows I could never be Zig Ziglar."

The young man nodded and said, "Yep, that's right."

We went ahead with the transaction. He got ready to do the paperwork. He picked up his pen and said, "Now what is your name?"

I said, "Well, I spell it Z-I-G-L-A-R."

He dropped his pen on the counter and said, "You *are* Zig Ziglar."

"Yes, I have been a long time," I said.

I want to make a very important point. The young man had a picture of me in his mind, and as far as that picture went, it was OK, because on occasion, I do jump up and down, and I do get kind of loud and exuberant and enthusiastic, but that picture he had of me was so narrow and shallow that it bore no resemblance to who I am and what I can do.

I have found that to be very, very true of people. Most people have a picture of themselves which is so narrow and so shallow that it bears no resemblance to who they are and what they can do. Most people have no earthly idea of what they can do because all they've ever been told is what they *cannot* do.

According to psychologist Shad Helmstetter, the average sixteen-year-old has been told no or "you can't do that" 17,000 times. You tell a youngster 17,000 times they can't do something, and they will begin to believe it. The picture is so incredibly important.

Most people have no earthly idea of what they can do because they don't know who they are. They do not know what they really want out of life because they do not know what's available for them. They can readily see where *you* could do it, but "Poor little old me, I could never do those things."

We want to work at changing the picture so that we can recognize just what is inside of us. To repeat myself again, man was designed for accomplishment—that's you, engineered for success, and endowed with the seeds of greatness. You are fearfully and wonderfully made.

There are some things you can't measure. You can measure the IQ, but you can't measure the heart. I talk to both the head and the heart because I like to get to your intelligence logically, but even more importantly, I like to get to you emotionally. Inside of us there is so much, but the picture is the key.

The picture I always had of myself was that I was a little guy from a little town who would struggle all of his life. When I was seventeen years old, getting ready to go off to the Navy back in World War II (some of you have heard about it; it's been in all the papers), my plan was to go off to war and come back to open a meat market in Yazoo City, Mississippi.

That's the picture that I had of myself. I never saw myself as having to have government assistance, but I did see myself as the little guy from the little town who would struggle all of his life. As a youngster, I was very small, and I did have that inferiority complex. That's what they called it in those days. Today they call it *poor self-image* and what have you, but the emphasis simply was that I could not do these things. The picture is important.

One time one of my children came home with a terrible report card. I was chastising him a little bit about it, and a big smile came on his face. He said, "Dad, let me ask you. Do you think this is heredity or environment?"

My environment as a youngster was a Depression environment. Survival was the issue of the day. Many of you are in a survival mode. We want to move first from survival to stability and from stability to success and from success to significance. That is the purpose, but that's going to take growth, and growth is a lifetime prospect.

I want to differentiate between personal growth and self-fulfillment. Self-fulfillment is the part of life that says, "Hooray for me, to heck with you. I'm going to win through intimidation if I have to, but I'm going to do it my way, and I'm going to look out for number one."

I can perhaps represent them in the world of athletics. It's the individual who becomes a bodybuilder. The typical bodybuilder spends an awful lot of time building those muscles and then spends an inordinate amount of time getting in front of the mirror and admiring his handiwork. But they're not altogether selfish: many of them will put on an undershirt and walk down Main Street so that we too can admire what they have done. They will even come in the restaurant where we are eating and casually sit in that Charles Atlas pose so we can admire them.

Please understand that there are exceptions to every rule. For example, Randy Webster is a trainer and a bodybuilder. He works with my son and did work with my daughter-in-law. He is genuinely interested in taking what he knows about bodybuilding and teaching somebody else. There's your difference. *That's* personal growth—the teacher who learns things for the purpose of teaching.

Self-fulfillment is the student who learns things so they can parade their knowledge. Maybe some day they'll get invited to appear on *Jeopardy*, and they can answer all of those questions, and then the world will admire them for their incredible insights and wisdom.

But when you get into these things, you begin to think, "I'm not the only fish in the pond. There are others, and I need to live with, work with, encourage other people." That is so important.

You go up in life not just by your own efforts but by what you can persuade others to do and teach others to do. You yourself have been helped by many people on many occasions.

You walk in my office today and you will see my Wall of Gratitude. There are nineteen people there who have had an impact on my life. If you're honest and really reflect on it, you've had a lot of people that have helped you to move up in your life. Like this old boy down home says, "Anytime you see a turtle on a fencepost, you can rest assured that sucker didn't get there by himself. He had some help along the way."

What are the benefits of team play? Two of my favorite football programs are at Penn State and Notre Dame. As far as I know, they're the only two major schools which do not put the names of the players on the jerseys. They go by numbers, so that big defensive tackle has a number, as does the outstanding quarterback. They function as a team. Well, we all know the success of those two teams.

Take Penn State, for example. If one of the players, a wide receiver, a running back, or a fullback, runs for a touchdown and does all those histrionics in the end zone—you know, throwing the ball up in the stands or throwing it over the goalpost or doing some of those silly dances—he might as well just head for the bench, because he is now officially out of the game. It is required that they simply hand the ball to one of the officials, run back to the huddle, and say, "Congratulations, fellows. Every last one of you did your job, and so the team was able to score."

What impact does this have on the individual? Check the record, and you will discover that for many years, both Notre Dame and Penn State have been at the top or real close to the top, certainly within the top five, of the teams that send players to the NFL.

You see, you have the individual with talent and ability, but you need to function in there as part of the team. I can tell you that one sour apple in a company can have a tremendously detrimental effect on the rest of the team, so this concept of team play becomes extraordinarily important.

Let me tell you first of all that it is a lifetime concept. Fifty-eight percent of the people in our society, when they finish their formal education, never read another meaningful book. On the other hand, those who make *Who's Who* read an average of twenty books a year. At the end of five years, one has read 100 books, gotten incredible additional information, stayed current and up-to-date, and is in a growth mode. When you're growing, you check your attitude. When you're learning things, that's when you are most excited.

In companies where they teach concepts and philosophies and people are growing, their rate of turnover is dramatically less than those who do not. *Fortune* magazine ran an article on an American company which for nine years was voted the number-one company, the most desirable place to work, in America. They discovered that it cost them one and one-half year's salary to replace a worker, to run the recruitment ads, and to train them, bring them up to speed. It cost them a year and a half salary every time a trained, productive individual left. So, you see, growth is important for the company, and it's important for the individual.

Let me get you to realize that the thoughts, ideas, and procedures in this book constitute an ongoing message. I don't necessarily finish a message in one particular chapter. I'm not concerned with that kind of literary structure. I'm concerned with delivering a message that will make a difference in your life.

I also want to encourage you to get your family to read this book, because that will put you all on the same page. You could even read it aloud to them. Over years, I've had lots of people tell me, "You know, there were plenty of times when my parents had me listen to Zig Ziglar. I have to tell you, I hated you. I'd say, 'Ma, do we have to read that Zig fellow again?'"

But across the board they have said, "You know, as I got old enough to even begin to understand what you were saying, I have always benefited from your ideas. I did have to admit that regardless of what you were saying, I felt better when you got through." This kind of activity floods the brain with endorphins, dopamine, norepinephrine, serotonin, and other neurotransmitters, so the physiological impact is there.

Why should we share with our family early on? According to a study done in Missouri, 65 percent of our working vocabulary has been acquired by the age of three. It's an established fact that people who teach you language teach you how to think. Since your thought precedes the action, that gets to be very, very important.

Now 80 percent of our character is formed by age five; 90 percent by the age of seven. Those first years are extremely important. And for those of you who think, "Shucks, my youngest child is forty-seven. Maybe it's too late for me," the beautiful thing is you can change. Whatever the situation is, you're not stuck with it. You can grow. You can change.

When I was a youngster, we obviously did not have cassette players. We did not have television. We didn't have a whole lot of other things. I had a mother with a fifth-grade education who was a magnificent philosopher, one of the wisest people that I have ever encountered.

Dad died when I was five, as I mentioned earlier, and six of us were too young to work, but Mom used to educate us by saying the same thing over and over. One of her favorites was "Willful waste makes woeful want." To this day, I am conscious of waste.

A number of years ago, when my son was a teenager, I was in the bathroom. I used to buy shampoo by the gallon, and then I would pour it into little bottles; that was the most economical way to do it.

Well, I was shaving and getting ready to take my shower, and I was transferring some of the shampoo from the gallon jug over to the little bottles. I spilled some of it there in the sink. So I reached down, wiped the shampoo up from the sink, and put it on my hair, and about that time my teenage son walked in. He said, "Dad, what happened to your hair?"

I told him what happened, and he just laughed. He said, "Well, Dad, nobody's ever going to accuse you of being wasteful."

I said, "Son, you know that nice old car you have standing out there in the driveway? It's there because we're careful about things like this."

My mom had all those sayings over and over. Another thing she used to say to us: "When a task is once begun, you leave it not until it's done." That was hammered into my mind many times, and I remember it, obviously, until this day. She often said, "Tell the truth until and tell it ever, costeth what it will; for he who hides the wrong he does, does the wrong thing still."

Probably the thing I'm most grateful for and proud of is that I'm consistent. Consistency is very important. Your word ought to be your bond. You should not need a written contract except for clarification.

I learned some things early on that did have a big influence on my life. For example, I milked cows when I was a youngster, eight years old. Just for your information, I have to tell you: cows don't give milk. You have to fight for every drop.

At lunch during school, I would come home, and I would move the cows from one spot to another so they could get better grass so we would have more milk.

Once I was in a big hurry to get back and play a couple of innings of softball, so I did it very sloppily. One of the cows got loose, got in this elderly lady's garden, and ate some turnip greens. I apologized profusely and told her how sorry I was and all that good stuff, and I really was sorry. But when I got home, my mama said, "Son, you have to do more than apologize. This lady sells turnip greens. You need to go to her and ask her to estimate how many turnip greens the cow ate, how many bunches that would represent, and you have to pay her for them."

So I went to her and said, "Tell me what it is, and I'll pay you." The lady estimated that there were about eight bunches, and in those days a bunch of turnip greens sold for a nickel. That's forty cents. Now that doesn't sound like a whole lot, except that in the grocery store where I worked, I made a nickel on the hour. That means I worked eight hours because I did not accept my responsibility of securing that gate.

Guess what I learned early on. I learned responsibility. I think that's important. Another little lesson I taught—and, you see, regardless of your age, I think this lesson is more needed today than ever before.

I was a Boy Scout. My instructions were, you go to the Scout meet, and then you come on home. Well, the schoolyard was next to the place where we held our Scout meeting, in the Episcopal church there in Yazoo City. A bunch of the kids decided to go over and play on the swings awhile. I went over there and played a few minutes, and then I headed home.

The next day, I got the report that some of the kids had stayed a little while longer and had destroyed some of the swings. My part of it was $1.15. I said, "Mom, that's not fair. I wasn't there when any of the damage was done."

She said, "Son, maybe that is true, but I have told you what to do and you do not do it, and many times when you're disobedient, there is a penalty that goes along with that." I have to tell you that $1.15 was a lot of money for me, although by then I was little older and was now making a dime an hour, so it was only a little less than twelve hours of work. But I guarantee you I listened much more carefully from that point on.

Lessons and philosophy. The reality is any kind of training that we give increases productivity—almost any kind of training. Remember the Hawthorne study? They turned the lights in this factory brighter, and productivity went up. Then they turned them down, and productivity went up temporarily.

Just about any kind of training will do that, but over a period of time, as it sets in and gets to be old hat, we revert back to form unless we as individuals grow and change.

That's where we like to believe we're different. We deal with the fact that you have to *be* before you can *do*, and you have to *do* before you can *have*. So we're going to look at the growth factor that will make a difference. When you reach a certain age, there are chemical changes that take place in the human body. As you know, we have a lot of pollution out there in the air, and when the chemical changes in the body meet the pollution in the air, it destroys the strength of the lenses in your glasses.

That happened to me a few years ago. So I went down to see my friendly optometrist, and he gave me all the tests, wrote the prescription, and said "See me next Tuesday; they'll be ready." Well, the following Tuesday I walked in, he put these new bifocals on me, and said, "OK, Zig, how do they feel?"

I said, "They feel good."

"They look good too. You're on your way."

My car was parked about fifteen or twenty feet outside of his front door. As I stepped out the front door in my new bifocals, I headed for my car. Now you're talking about a high-stepping dude. Old Zig was really picking them up and putting them down. I didn't realize that until I drew abreast of the car. There I was, my right leg up there about three and a half feet, and I saw the reflection in the window.

You know how you feel when you do something that's not overly bright: you look around for fear that everybody in town has been watching you. I looked around right quick. Nobody was paying me the least bit of attention, but realizing how utterly ridiculous I must have looked, I could not help it. I burst out laughing, and then I got excited. That day, for the first time in my life, I realized what I do. Basically, I go around this country, and other countries as well, fitting people with new glasses, because if we're going to change that picture, we have to also adapt to those new glasses that will make a difference.

I want to emphasize that these are not rose-colored glasses. I've said it before; I've said it a number of times. Life is tough, but when you're tough on yourself, then life will infinitely easier on you. I also want to emphasize that neither are they *woes*-colored glasses. Many people walk around looking like the picture on their driver's license, acting somewhat like the cruise director for the Titanic, like somebody's licked all the red off of their candy.

No, these are not woes-colored glasses. These are vision glasses, which will enable you to see further and understand more. Vision glasses are enormously important. Somebody asked Helen Keller what would be worse than being blind. Without hesitation, she said, "It would be infinitely worse to have perfect eye-sight and no vision than the other way around."

In his last year, somebody asked Albert Schweitzer, "How goes it, Dr. Schweitzer?" He said, "My sight grows dim, but my vision is clearer than ever."

Solomon said, "My people perish for a lack of a vision." I believe with all my heart that's one of the basic problems, not only individually, but that we as a society and many companies and families have. Their vision is limited, and that is unfortunate. It is even tragic.

Again, Oliver Wendell Holmes was right when he said, "It's tragic, the loss of our natural resources, but what is even more tragic is the fact that the average American goes to their grave with their music still in them." All of us have those songs in us.

Nat King Cole was on the West Coast early on. He got his career started as a piano player. One night the singer did not show. The club owner said, "Where's the singer?"

Nat King Cole said, "He's not here. He's sick."

"No singer, no money," the owner said. That's the night Nat King Cole became a singer, and of course the rest is history.

Now you might not be able to carry a tune, but you have a song inside of you, and the purpose of these messages is to get the song out, whatever it might be, so that you can sing that song.

You know what I believe about myself? I tell people this, and sometimes they look at me as if I'm just whistling Dixie. I honestly believe that I'm at least five, maybe ten years away from reaching my peak. I feel better, more energetic, stronger, better informed than I've ever felt in my life. The research I'm doing clearly indicates that if you remain active physically and mentally—and I still read an average of three hours a day—your creativity substantially increases, because you have accessed all of the accumulated information and knowledge you've acquired over the years.

I recently signed a contract to do a daily newspaper column for seven years. We're in thirty-two papers now, and if you call your local paper, maybe we'll get in your paper as well. They insisted on a seven-year renewal, so that's fourteen years. I believe in those long-range goals. I really do.

A lot of times people ask me, "Do you ever think about retirement?" I say, "Yes, and I said no a long time ago." You might not know this, but the only times retirement is mentioned in the Bible, it is always as a punishment. I hope God is not ready to punish me for a while at any rate; I have so many things I want to do. I'm ready to go when he's ready for me, but I also have a lot of things I would like to get done.

That retirement baloney got started in Germany in the 1870s, when Bismarck was the chancellor. He noticed one day that virtually every one of his powerful enemies was sixty-five and older. He persuaded the German legislature to pass legislation making sixty-five the mandatory retirement age. Now he neglected to explain to everybody what he was doing, but in one stroke of the pen, he eliminated the overwhelming majority of all of his enemies who had power, judgment, wisdom, influence, contacts, money. For some reason, a lot of other countries said, "That's a good idea; let's do that too." As a result, in many cases, we're putting people out to pasture as they hit their peak. I think it's a tragic mistake.

Many people are so age-conscious. I was doing a radio talk show a few months ago, and this lady called in. It was one of those question-and-answer deals. She was almost crying. She said, "I'm fifty-five years old. I've never done anything with my life, and now it's too late."

I said, "Ma'am, did you say you were fifty-five?"

"Yes, I am," she said.

"You're just a spring chicken," I said. "As a matter of fact, does you mama know where you are?" She got so tickled, and the rest of the time we talked about solutions.

Many people go through life whining. I really ought to carry some cheese with me so we can have whine and cheese. They tell me those things go together.

I have an idea right now that you're smiling because we've been telling a little funny or two, and you're kind of interested in what I'm going to say. As a matter of fact, you've invested your money, so that's proof that you're interested in what I'm going to say.

I'd like to talk about the power of the spoken word, because the spoken word has the power to influence in an unbelievable manner and degree. Years ago, somebody said one picture is worth a thousand words. That individual never really read the Declaration of Independence or the Bill of Rights. They've not read Lincoln's Gettysburg Address or the Twenty-Third Psalm or prayed the Lord's Prayer.

See, those are words. They're just words, but they're words that have impacted millions and millions of people. Words can make you break out in hilarious laughter. You've heard it 101 different times.

The book *Anguished English* contains this entry written by actual students:

Socrates was a famous Greek teacher who went around giving people advice. They killed him. Socrates died from an overdose of wedlock. After his death, his career suffered a dramatic decline.

Now, you know, when you read something like that, you can't help but get tickled. When you read something like that, it does have an impact, an influence on your thinking.

Charles Osgood said, "Compared to the spoken word, a picture is a pitiful thing indeed." You think about these words. Patrick Henry said, "Give me liberty or give me death," and a nation united and fought for their independence. Lincoln said, "Four score and seven years ago," and a nation was reunited. Churchill said, "There will always be an England," and the country was lifted by its bootstraps. FDR said, "The only thing we have to fear is fear itself," and the Depression era got a glimpse of hope. Martin Luther King said, "I have a dream," and because of it many people dream today who did not dream before. Rosa Parks said, "My feet hurt," and because of those few words, an entire people stood up and marched forward.

Words can be so enormously important. Many years ago, I told a beautiful young girl, "I love you." A few weeks later, she said to me, "I love you." Two and a half years later, the preacher said, "I now pronounce you man and wife." A little over two years later, the doctor said, "It's a girl, Mr. Ziglar." Now those are words that can lift you up.

A youngster in a California school had all kinds of problems, came from a dysfunctional family, and was failing in everything. They put computers in there, and he had a knack for computers. All of a sudden, he started to improve, and in every area of life his grades got dramatically better. Somebody asked him, "What has happened?" He said, "Well, my computer calls me Clarence. My classmates call me stupid."

Words can make a difference. Dr. Les Carter, at the world-famous Minirth-Meier Clinic, talked about the impact of words. I was concerned about this, and I said, "Is there a correlation between violent language and violence itself?" Dr. Carter said, "I have never worked with an abuse situation that didn't follow a pattern of verbal abuse before physical abuse. Additionally, the more one cusses, the less sensitive to the nature of their own behavior they become."

The Bible says, "Thou shall not curse a deaf man." Why not? They can't hear. It's obviously because of the damage it does to you, as it destroys the vessel in which it is stored, and that's important. The way people talk is the best indication of how they think.

The most powerful instrument for influencing a person's thought process is the language you use on them and they use on themselves. That's the reason I always use so much adult language, like *dedication*, *responsibility*, *commitment*, *discipline*, and things like that, and a lot of four-letter words, like *good* and *best* and *real* and *fair* and *hope* and *love*. I have to confess, every once in a while I slip the F word in on folks, because I believe that faith is enormously important.

The language we use can have a substantial impact on a person's life. The language we use on ourselves can have an even greater impact. Again, the most important opinion you have is the opinion you have of yourself. I'm not talking about a super-inflated ego. You know, conceit's that weird disease that makes everybody sick except the person who has it. It's kind of like the rooster who thinks the sun comes up so that it's time for him to crow. That is not what I'm talking about.

How powerful can words be? A few years ago, I was speaking in Marion, Indiana. It was a four-hour seminar. I did it on Tuesday night. When I got home on the weekend, I had a letter from a lady who was there, and she said, "Mr. Ziglar, I was there on Tuesday night. I had just gotten back from Colorado on a rafting trip. It was one of the most magnificent experiences of my life. It was really wonderful. We would raft down the river, and as the sun was beginning to set, we would pull off to a flat spot. We would build our campfire. We would cook our dinner, and then we would go up a few hundred more feet so we could get a better view.

"The rarefied air up there, and the clarity—we could look at the stars and the moon, it was incredible. I looked at the magnificent universe, and then the next morning we'd get up and go down to the streams, and the wildlife would be coming there to take their morning drink. The whole thing was so awesome that I thought of myself as being absolutely nothing and contemplated suicide.

"That evening, on Tuesday evening, you quoted St. Augustine." Many years ago, in 399 A.D., he said, "Man travels hundreds of miles to gaze at the broad expanse of the ocean. He looks with awe at the heavens above. He stares in wonderment at the fields and the mountains and the rivers and the streams, and then he passes himself by without a thought, God's most amazing creation."

She said, "When you quoted St. Augustine, I realized what I was."

When people look at themselves and what's important with this pair of glasses you're being fitted with, they will also reverse themselves. They will look inside and let you see some things. You're going to be astonished at what is already there.

The power of the word truly is awesome. We had a young man named Samuel Akwasi Sarpong who came to our three-day "Born to Win" seminar in Dallas. He's from the Ashanti tribe in Ghana.

The Ashanti tribe, which is by far the largest tribe in Ghana, has the practice of naming their children based on the day of the week on which they're born. They have a given name and a last name. The middle name is their Ashanti name. His Ashanti name is Akwasi, and *akwasi* in his language means *godly, gentle, peace-loving*, and *kind*. By coincidence, the young man is a Christian minister.

The babies who are born on Wednesday are named Kwaku. *Kwaku* means *mean, violent, aggressive, quick-tempered*. In Ghana, over 50 percent of all crime is committed by those who were born on Wednesday. You see, names, words, language are extraordinarily important.

Wendell Johnson wrote a book entitled *People in Quandaries*. It's based on studies done on reservations in America. He started with two reservations and noticed something rather peculiar. Then he expanded it to many other reservations. They discovered there was not a single, full-blooded Indian who was raised on the reservation and taught the Indian languages and dialects who stuttered.

They checked the languages, and then they understood why none of them stuttered. It was because in none of the Indian languages or dialects was there a word for *stutter*. If there's no word for *stutter*, how are you going to stutter? You see, there are no instructions. There's no picture.

Words paint pictures, and then we go to work to complete those pictures. Bill Glass says that 90 percent of the people who are incarcerated in our prisons today were repeatedly told by their parents, "One of these days, you're going to end up in jail."

Jim Sundberg is a friend of mine, a former Golden Gloves catcher in the major leagues. Jim Sundberg was doing a prison crusade with Bill Glass one day, and during one of the breaks, they were standing aside and talking. Jim said, "Bill, when I was a youngster, over and over my dad kept saying to me, 'You keep throwing that ball like that, son, you'll be major leaguer some day. You keep hustling like that, and some day you'll be a major leaguer. You keep swinging the bat that way, one of these days you're going to be a major leaguer.'" He said, "It was planted in my mind early on. I'm exactly where my dad told me I was going to be."

A prisoner was standing close by. He softly shook his head and said, "Well, you know, same thing happened to me. I'm exactly where my dad told me I was going to be."

The power of the word is absolutely incredible. Yet so much of the input is negative. What do we say to our kids? We call them the terrible twos when they're really the terrific twos, tremendous threes, fantastic fours, fabulous fives, sensational sixes.

How many times do we hear somebody say, "You never do you anything right. You're always late. You never look nice. You're just plain dumb. You'll never amount to anything. You're just like your father"? We hear that sort of stuff when we really need the good, clean, the pure, the powerful, the positive in there every day.

I was in Atlanta in my office many years ago. A young man came in with three beautiful little stair-step girls. He introduced them—"This is the one that won't eat. This is the one that won't mind her mother. This is the one who cries all the time"—not realizing he was giving them very specific instructions.

I was up in Nashville on the way down to the gate to catch a plane. I passed a mother and her three-year-old child, and since Adam and Eve there has never been a child who has walked at exactly the pace the parent wanted them to walk. Well, this little guy was dragging his heels, and the mother turned to him and said, "Come on, stupid, we're going to miss the plane."

I was in a cafeteria in Dallas, and a little girl was crying. A grandmotherly lady bent over her and said,

"What's the matter, honey?" Her dad spoke up and said, "She's mean, that's what. She's just plain mean."

I was out in Stockton, California. I was doing my jog. I ran past a grandmother and her little granddaughter, about five, six years old, beautiful little girl. I'll tell you just how pretty she was: she compares favorably to my own grandchildren. If that doesn't say something, I don't know what would.

As I ran past them, the only thing I heard was these words: "They'll put you in jail for that." Can you imagine?

Had I the opportunity to talk with that man in Atlanta, the man in Dallas, the mother up in Nashville, the grandmother in Stockton, I would have said to them, "If you want to destroy their self-image, if you want to discourage them, if you want to consign them to the failure heaps in life, if you want to give them higher hills to climb, you keep on doing exactly what you are doing." The same rule applies between husband and wife and employer and employee.

As you've undoubtedly already noticed, I put it all together—personal life, family life, and business life, your physical, your mental, and your spiritual sides—because you're a complete human being, not just part of a human being.

The sad thing is that there are so many people who are unaware of what they're doing. It's just gotten to be a habit. If they were to keep an open recording going in their house and listen at the end of the day to some of the things they're saying, they would be absolutely astonished.

What difference do words and attitude make? I was twenty-five years old. I was the youngest divisional supervisor in the sixty-six-year history of a very large cookware company. When I was promoted, I immediately encountered difficulty. In direct sales, the field manager is the key, because they're in daily contact with the troops, they do the weekly sales meetings, they do all of the training sessions, and I had four field managers.

In that first month, one of them had a heart attack. One of them cut his big toe almost all the way off. He was in the hospital for twenty days and on crutches for the next three months. The third one had an integrity problem: his people lost confidence in him, and they quit in droves. The fourth one had been promoted prematurely because there was no one else available. A division that was going gangbusters one month was going kaput the next month.

Some of my friends started the rumor that the company was very unhappy with me because I just couldn't cut the mustard, as we'd say in those days. I couldn't handle this bigger job, this bigger responsibility. Now you're talking about a pity party. Old Zig had one, a protracted one.

I was muttering, "It's not my fault. I didn't have anything to do with that heart attack. I didn't have anything to do with cutting his toe off. I didn't have anything to do with that inexperience. I didn't have anything to do with that integrity problem. I'm the good guy. Why are they trying to crucify me?" Business kept getting worse for some strange reason.

Walking down the streets of Knoxville, Tennessee, I saw a book in the window. It was called *The Power of Positive Thinking,* Dr. Norman Vincent Peale. I picked that sucker up. I said, "Boy, if anybody ever needs to be a positive thinker right now, if there's anybody that needs help, boy, it is me." I devoured that book, which Dr. Peale had taken the time to write expressly to me and for me.

Every page, almost every paragraph, it said, "Now Zig, now Zig, Zig, Zig," over and over, and I was astonished that he had been able to personalize it to the degree that he had. He agreed with me completely. He said, "You're right. You're not responsible for that heart attack. You're not responsible for the integrity problem or the cut-off toe or the inexperience. You're not responsible for any of those things, but, Zig, you are responsible for you and your attitude. Now quit your griping, put your imagination to work, start thinking. How can you capitalize on this? How can you make it an asset instead of a liability?"

That was a dramatic turnaround. Nothing had changed out there, but everything changed in here. You see, the way you change others is, don't even try. You change *you*. The way you change your circumstances is change *you*. The way you do things better is become better yourself. That is the key.

What happened then was very simple. Shad Helmstetter says you can't change from a negative mind-set to a positive mind-set without changing from negative talking to positive talking.

To do that, you must change the input from negative to positive. Generally we extract the last major deposit in our thinking and in our attitudes and in our action. We simply recall the last deposit.

Let me tell you again. Input determines your outlook, your outlook determines your output, and your output determines your future. See if you can do something about your input.

If I were to walk in your home with a pail of garbage and dump it on your living-room floor, we'd have serious trouble fast. You'd either get your gun and say, "Now, Ziglar, you clean it up" or you'd call the law and you'd have me arrested. Or you'd whoop up on me.

We could clean it up with some good cleaner and remove all traces of it ever being there, but everything that goes in your mind is going to be there in some shape or form. You don't forget it. It just gets buried over a period of time.

One of the things that will happen as you listen to this is the fact that you will, over a period of time, become so conscious of what goes into your mind that you will catch yourself asking, "If I read this, am I going to be better off or worse off? If I watch this particular television show or movie, am I really going to be more likely to get the things in life I want, or is it going to be a detriment to me?" Yes, what goes in your mind is very, very important.

We have so many negatives. We call them stoplights when in reality they're go lights. They're put there to make traffic go. When we have a wreck, somebody says call the wrecker when need the tow truck. You've already had the wreck.

Incredibly enough, they bring out a loaf of bread, and the average person calls the first slice the end. Every loaf of bread I've ever seen in my life had two beginnings.

I challenge you: if you want to have fun and somebody wants directions, send them down to the go light. In a restaurant, ask the waiter or waitress, "I'd like the beginning slice of bread." They're going to look at you like, "Now there's a weird individual," but I can guarantee you it will make a difference. The power of the word can be measured in so many cases, in so many ways.

A number of years ago, when *The Dallas Times Herald* was in publication, there was an article concerning a study done at the University of Pittsburgh. They called me and asked me what I thought about it. I said, "I think it's a valid study." They said, "You mean, you believe it's right." I said, "Absolutely, that study's been done half a dozen times. I don't know why they keep on doing it."

The study showed that tall men and women do better in the business world than do short men and women. They said, "You believe that?"

"Why certainly, I believe it, and let me tell you why that is true. It has nothing whatever to do involving the distance between your heel and your head. It has nothing to do with the size of the storage place, because they basically are all about the same size. It has everything to do with what you put in it."

Tell me if you're guilty of this. Have you ever been lost? I do not mean confused, but I mean you're in a strange neighborhood and you just flat are lost. You know, Daniel Boone never was lost, but he was confused once for about a week.

Now you're lost. You don't whether to go north, south, east, or west. You see some kids playing on the school ground or on the corner or in somebody's yard. You go over there, and you ask a question.

Here's my question to you: which one of the kids do you ask? The biggest or tallest. It might be the dumbest kid in town. He might know nothing about how to get from here to there, but you ask the biggest or the tallest for one very simple reason: lifetime conditioning.

How many times have you been guilty of this? Somebody introduces you to their child. If the child is average or above average in height, you'll say, "My, what a fine-looking young man" or "What a fine-looking young woman." What about shorty? "Oh, isn't he cute?" or "Isn't she cute?"

I have a cute little dog at home, and you can have cute puppies, but have you ever seen a cute university president or a cute admiral or a cute general or a cute CEO of a major corporation? You don't relate greatness with cuteness, but that word has been ingrained, so when a small person comes in, many times that's our attitude towards them, and it permeates them over a period of time.

I love what Oliver Wendell Holmes said—brilliant jurist, brilliant writer. He was five feet tall. Somebody asked him one time, "Judge Holmes, how does it feel to be small in a society where men and women both are taller and bigger than you are?" He had a great sense of humor and showed lot of wisdom when he said, "I feel kind of like a dime must feel when thrown in with a bunch of nickels. Half as big, worth twice as much."

What am I getting at? I'm getting at an attitude. I'm getting at the fact that words really do make a difference. In the make-believe world, television and Hollywood, profanity and vulgarity might be in, but not in the real world. I've never heard of a young girl going home and saying, "Dad, you have to let me go out with this fellow. I'm telling you he has the filthiest mouth I have ever heard in my life."

I've never heard of a director of personnel going to the president and saying, "I want to hire this person right here. He can tell the filthiest and dirtiest jokes you've ever heard. I mean, he will have an impact on our company."

Let me tell you the reality. I've never heard of anybody advancing because of vile, filthy language. I've heard a lot of them who never had a chance to get ahead because of it.

A number of years ago, I'd spoken for one of the major companies in America for a couple of years, and they asked me who I would recommend for next year. Obviously I recommended me again. They wanted my best recommendation, so you have to be realistic about it.

Anyhow, they said, "No, Zig, come on. We've had you several times now, and you always do a great job for us, but tell us about somebody else." I suggested a fellow who happened to be a friend of mine.

They said, "Does he have any tapes?"

"Yes, he does."

"Tell him to send us a couple, and let us listen to him." He sent them the tapes. They called him and told him they could not use him. He obviously wanted to know why. They said, "You have a couple of stories in there that just won't fit in our organization."

"That's no problem," he said, "I'll just take those stories out."

They said to him, "We were really looking for someone who had never put the stories in there in the first place."

See, your language is dramatically important. That's the reason we talk about it so much. Suppose a parent were to say, "You keep performing like that, and someday you'll be the president of your own company. You keep studying like that, and someday you'll win a college scholarship. You keep treating people like that, and you'll have friends everywhere."

That, I believe, is the proper use of language. Using things that really do make a difference in people's life.

Truth not only is stranger than fiction, but in most cases, it's funnier than fiction. A number of years ago my brother, Judge Ziglar, who was also a speaker, was going through Charlotte, North Carolina. It was a cold, rainy, winter evening, and he was in the old airport. They used to have a chocolate-chip cookie machine there. You could smell those chocolate-chip cookies for blocks away.

My brother could handle anything except temptation, so he got close enough to smell, and he went up and bought himself a dozen of them. (They were small, so it's not quite as bad as it sounded.) He went into the waiting area, and there were two seats left, side by side. There was a lady on one side, so he proceeded.

He had his hat on and his topcoat and his raincoat and his briefcase, and all of the paraphernalia that goes with traveling. He put all of those things down, and as he turned around to sit down, when he looked back over, he saw a hand coming out of his chocolate-chip cookies. He thought, "Well, you know, at least she could have asked. Of course, I have a dozen, so it's OK."

He reached over, and he got himself a cookie, and the lady looked at him kind of funny. In a minute or two, she got another one, and he got another one. She got another one, he got another one, and he got the last cookie. Then she picked the empty sack up, dumped the crumbs in her hand, popped them in her mouth, and about that time, the call came for her flight.

Well, she got up, and as she walked past him, she gave him a look that would skin the hide off of a billy goat. He thought, "Boy, that is one more nervy woman. These are strange people up here."

About ten minutes later, his call came. He got up, slipped on his topcoat, put on his hat, and underneath his hat was a bag of chocolate-chip cookies.

Now if you ever meet a woman who said, "You can't believe that strange dude I saw in Charlotte, North Carolina," that was my brother that she would be talking about.

Several years ago, I got a letter from a gentleman in Toronto, Canada. The letter contained a substantial check, and he said, "Mr. Ziglar, I know you don't do counseling, but I have young a friend who's destroying his health, losing his family, and I believe you are the only person he will listen to. He has great respect for you. If you will give us an hour, I will fly the two of us to Dallas. The check is yours if you'll spend an hour with us."

The first thing I thought is, "Man, isn't it wonderful to have a friend like that." So I sent the check back and told him to come on down. The young man's name was Steve Walker. They walked in, and we started our dialogue.

I said, "I understand your boss is your hero."

"That's right," he said, "the most successful man that I know."

"I also understand that you're a hard worker."

"Yes, I am a hard worker."

Let me tell you just how hard he was working because his boss was a hard worker. The young man was leaving every morning at 6:00 to go to work. Drove thirty miles. He got home, generally speaking, after 10:00 at night. On several occasions, he literally went to sleep driving. His health was deteriorating, his family was coming apart, but he was really following this guy who was his boss.

"Well, now," I said, "we have to look at success and see what it is. I'd like for you to tell me what you consider success to be."

We talked, and when we finally got through, he agreed that anybody who was happy and healthy and at least reasonably prosperous and secure, who had friends, peace of mind, good family relationships, and hope that the future was going to be better, was a successful man.

I said, "Let's do something that most people never do. Let's evaluate where we are in pursuit of what we want versus where we think we might be." I said to the young man, "For example, we know that if I divide an audience of salespeople exactly half in two, and they're all salespeople, with the same abilities, same experience, and same territory, selling the same products, but one half keeps precise records about the people they call on, what happened, and how they can improve on the next one, they will sell dramatically more than the other one will.

"On weight loss, people who keep exact records of what they eat, I mean every bite, will lose weight faster and will keep it off longer than those who say, 'I don't really eat that much.' It depends on what they call *much*. Most people on a diet are in denial, and as you know, denial is just a river in Egypt as far as a lot of people are concerned.

"So," I said, "let's talk about your boss, and let's see how he measures up with your picture of success. First of all, how happy is your boss?"

"I don't really think he's happy."

"Why do you say that?"

"First of all, I almost never see him smile. I don't think I've heard him laugh a half a dozen times, and on top of that, he has ulcers."

"Based on what you just told me," I said, "we have to give him a failing grade on the happiness part and on the health. If he has ulcers, that raises a failure there at this particular moment. You get ulcers not because of what you eat but because of what's eating you, so that means he doesn't have peace of mind.

"Now I've asked you one question, and three of the eight things that you consider to be success he doesn't have. Tell me about how prosperous he is."

"Oh, man, he is rolling in the dough. He's making more all the time."

"Well, OK. On the prosperity bit, we will give him a big old plus. Now let me ask you: how secure is your boss?"

Now understand he's thinking mostly financial security. He said, "Well, he's as secure as money can make him."

"Well now," I said, "we had an ex-governor worth over $100 million, and he went bankrupt. How does your boss compare to him?"

"Oh, he doesn't have that much money."

"We had an industrialist in this area worth over half a billion, and he went bankrupt. He couldn't compare with him, could he?"

"No."

So I said, "Really, the financial security—would it be fair to say that as far as that's concerned, there is a legitimate question?"

Yes, things happen. Actually only nineteen of the top 100 corporations in America in 1,900 are still in business today. So we do know that things change there.

"Tell me, how many friends does your boss have?"

He thought a minute. He said, "I don't think he has any. Actually, I'm not his friend. I just admire him a lot. To tell you the truth, the guy is somewhat of a jerk."

"OK, then we'll give him a failing grade on that one." I said, "Tell me about his family relationships."

"Well, his wife's divorcing him."

"We kind of have to give him a big old X on that one. Tell me about his hope for the future."

"He thinks he has a great future, but I'm beginning to think that maybe he doesn't after all."

"In other words, we could put an honest question mark on the hope part."

"Yes, I think we could."

"Now, let's take a little inventory of the eight things you consider to be success. He gets a plus on one, he gets a minus on five, and a maybe on two of them. Let me ask you a question. Based on this actual, factual exploration of your admiration for the most successful man you know, would you swap places with him?"

The young man sat there, kind of stunned, for quite a few seconds, then slowly he stood up. He extended his hand, indicating the interview was over.

Now let me ask you a question. Would you exchange everything you hold dear to have more bucks in the bank? I daresay that nobody would be willing to do that. The good news is you don't have to. If you go for quality of life first and if you plan the other things, then they're far more likely to happen as well. The better balanced you are, ultimately, the more income you're going to have.

Life cannot always be in perfect balance every day and every week, but when we keep our records and our inventory, if we get completely out of balance and keep saying, "Next week I'll do better," that's called your attention. You say, "Hey, this week is the next week I was talking about last week." Tomorrow really does come, and we need to think about that.

If you're going to achieve all the things you want, you have to see yourself in that category. The picture you have of yourself is enormously important. You cannot be one kind of person and another kind of performer. You have to have a picture of yourself, and you cannot, as Dr. Joyce Brothers said, consistently perform in a manner which is inconsistent with the way you see yourself.

I met the young man, Steve Walker, again a couple of years ago at one of the seminars, and he gave me this picture. His family is well together. They've added a member of the family. That's what I call real growth.

He got an entirely different job. He's making more money than he was making when he was killing himself working himself to death. He said, "Thank you for helping to make this possible." The best way is the right way, folks.

For twenty-four years of my adult life, by choice, I weighed well over 200 pounds. I say "by choice" because I've never accidentally eaten anything. It's always a choice. If I choose to eat too much, than I've chosen to weigh too much.

Over those years, I tried every kind of diet known to man. I tried the thirty-day diet, and lost a month. I tried dieting religiously: I quit eating in church. I can tell you this about dieting. You need to stay away from cottage cheese. A lot of people don't know it, but that's the most fattening food in existence. Now I have no scientific evidence to validate that, but I've noticed in world travel that nobody but fat folks eat the stuff, so you draw your own conclusions. One thing I did discover that was positive is that my body retains ice cream. So I knew that I had to do something.

Twenty-three years ago, I got on a sensible eating and exercise program. Up until then, my idea of exercise was simply to fill the tub, take a bath, pull the plug, and fight the current. That's not really much of an exercise program.

The reality was that eating too much wasn't my problem. I had a picture of myself: I'm a fat boy. I'm a fat man. When my youngest daughter was eighteen months old, I told her to call me "fat boy." She didn't know what she was doing. She would laugh because I would laugh on the outside, but on the inside it was an entirely different matter.

I knew I was a fat boy, and it hurt. I could look in the mirror, and I could tell. I had a picture of me laying out on the diving board of the swimming pool—at least part of me was on the diving board. I saw myself as a fat boy, and as long as I saw myself as a fat boy, it didn't make any difference how much weight I lost; it was coming right back: it will come back 100 percent of the time until the picture changes. You have to see yourself where you want to be.

One of the most amazing and dramatic stories that I've ever heard is the story of Victor Serebriakoff. When Victor Serebriakoff was age sixteen, his teacher said to him, "You're a dunce, Victor. You're never going to finish school. Why don't you drop out and get a job? At least be able to support yourself."

He dropped out of school, and for nearly sixteen years, he was an itinerant. He went everywhere, did everything, served in the Army, and a host of other things. But every morning Victor would get up, he'd look in the mirror, and he would shave the dunce that looked back at him. He would dress that dunce. He would take that dunce to work. He would think as a dunce. He would perform as a dunce, and he would receive a dunce's wages.

At age thirty-one, for whatever reason, they did a psychological evaluation on him. The results came back, and with tremendous excitement, they went to Victor and said, "Victor, I don't know whoever told you you're a dunce, and I don't know why you think you are, because the scientific evidence is compulsive. There's zero doubt that we are in error. You, sir, are not a dunce. You have an IQ of 161. You, sir, are a genius."

They didn't tell him anything else—no new information, except the greatest information of all: you're not a dunce; you're a genius. Now he looks in the mirror and shaves a genius. He dresses a genius. He goes to work as a genius. He thinks as a genius. He performs as a genius, and the bottom line is that Victor Serebriakoff has a number of books out. He has several patents to his credit. He is a very successful businessman and owns several businesses. One year he was the international chairman of Mensa, and you have to have an IQ of 140 just to get in there.

He had the information and the knowledge and the IQ all the time, but he had the wrong picture. The wrong picture was there because of the input into his mind. When you change the picture, that's when everything changes.

Linda Isaacs is down here from Italy, Texas. Linda is African-American. She's a dwarf. They evaluated her when she was just a little girl, four years old. They discovered she couldn't learn. They put her in a school when the time came, but they were really nice to her, and they told the teacher, "Linda's a cute little girl. Her classmates will all call her Shorty. She's very friendly, easy to get along with, won't give you a moment's trouble, but don't worry about trying to teach her anything, because she can't learn."

They passed her from the first to the second to the third grade. They said, "We don't want her to have to make a new set of friends every year. Just let her go on through." She graduated from high school functioning at the first-grade level.

What about her future? She was a member of a minority race, a dwarf. What were her chances? Very slim, except her mother was getting on up in years. She had an older sister who lived right here in Dallas. Her mother brought her to Dallas to live with her older sister. She took her down to Goodwill Industries, where she met Carol Clapp. Carol Clapp put her through this intensive two-week acclimation school and discovered something: Linda could learn some things.

For years Linda had been saying, "Linda can't learn. Linda can't learn. Linda can't learn." Sure enough, she was right. Now all of a sudden Linda's saying, "Hey, Linda can learn. Linda can learn. Linda can learn."

A year later, she was answering the telephone, checking the payroll, and functioning almost as a secretary. She learned more in a year than she had learned in the previous eighteen years.

Please do not read anything into this which I'm not saying. If there's brain damage, folks, that's a different matter. There are some cases where this is not going to work, but in every case, there will be improvement if we change the input and make it positive and upbeat while at the same time making it a realistic picture.

I want to tell you again: Your input determines your outlook, your outlook determines your output, and your output determines your future. The opinion you have of yourself and the opinion others have of you can make a big difference.

The most moving story I've ever heard about changing the picture is told by Brian Harbour in his beautiful book *Rising above the Crowd*. When little Ben Hooper was born all those years ago in the foothills of East Tennessee, little boys and girls who had no idea who their daddies were ostracized. They were treated horribly.

By the time he was three years old, the other kids in that little East Tennessee community wouldn't play with him. Parents were saying idiotic things like, "What's a boy like that doing playing with our kids?" as if the child had anything at all to do with his own birth.

When he was six years old, they put him in first grade—no kindergarten—and they gave him a little desk. All the kids had desks. At recess he stayed at his desk and studied. The other kids went out and played. At lunch he took his little sack lunch and went off and ate by himself. The other kids ate together. He had an extraordinarily tough childhood.

When he was twelve years old, a new preacher came to that little church in the foothills of East Tennessee. Almost immediately little Ben started hearing about what a wonderful man he was, how nonjudgmental he was, how when he was with you, he was *with* you: he gave you his undivided attention. He had that charisma when he walked in a room. Spirits were automatically lifted. He was very popular in that little community.

Little Ben had never been to church a day in his life. One Sunday, though, he decided to go. He got there late, and he left early. He did not want to attract any attention at all, but for the first time in that child's life, he caught just a glimpse of hope.

My good friend Dr. John Maxwell says, "If there's hope in the future, there's power in the present." I believe if there is that hope—and that's the purpose of this book, it's to give hope to every individual, whether you're a John Johnson or a Linda Isaacs or any one of the other people that I've been talking about—if we can give that individual hope, then they're going to take some action.

The question is how do you change the picture? Over the years, I've asked audiences all over the world to identify the qualities they would like to see in their boss, or if you're a boss, what qualities you would like to see in your employees.

Now here's something very important. I hope you have a pen. Look at this list. Go down it, and ask yourself, is that quality an attitude, or is it a skill? Write it down either an A or an S next to the word.

Honest	Decisive
Intelligent	Focused
Goals	Disciplined
Organized	Persistent
Responsible	Positive mental attitude
Commitment	Team player
Punctual	Energetic
Self-starter	Competent
Optimistic	Self-image
Enthusiastic	Common sense
Motivated	

These words will be familiar (except for the last: common sense) because I was going exactly down the list of qualities that you put to work when you go to the day-before-vacation attitude.

Here is the second list of words. Again, mark each one: is it an attitude or a skill?

Manners   Respectful
Gratitude   Caring
Teachable   Affectionate
Dependable   Supportive
Pride   Sincere
Diligent   Attentive
Thrifty   Personable
Resourceful   Open-minded
Extra-miler   A good-finder
Sober   Educated
Loyal

Now do the same thing with this list.

Passion   Authoritative
Convictions   Self-control
Encourager   Fair
Vision   Communicator
Faith   Consistent
Wisdom   Creative
Courage   Knowledgeable
Confident   Humor
Humble   A good listener
Smart   Teacher
Hard worker   Integrity

Do those words refer to attitudes or skills?
    I'd like to add a couple more:
    Service attitude   Obedience

Those are words that people in modern society don't get overly enthusiastic about. Let me share a story with you.

Notre Dame coach Lou Holtz is a good friend of mine. I've had the privilege of speaking to his team. He told me something that absolutely fascinates me. At the table there were student assistants, student managers, and a couple of assistant coaches. Every few minutes, one of the assistant coaches or Lou would say something, and a student manager would hop up, and in a dead run without hesitation, they would be off to do whatever he had been or she had been told to do. None of these student managers that I saw had more than three bites of dinner.

Lou told me that in the freshman year, they have roughly 250 that come in and want to be student managers. By the end of their senior year, approximately forty of them are left. Lou said when he travels the country, and he bumps into somebody and they say, "Coach, when I was at Notre Dame, for four years I was a student manager," he always has the same question to ask of them: "What company are you running today?" Or "what company are you the vice-president or president of?"

Almost never does he have them say anything but, "Well, I'm the CEO of—." Or "I own my business, and last year we did phenomenally."

Why would that be? Two big things, really: obedience. You have to learn to obey before you can learn to lead. Service attitude is also important. God himself said, "He who would be the greatest among you must become the servant of all."

Let's see if we can go back and tie all of this together with that Ben Hooper story. Little Ben Hooper went to church one day. He caught a glimpse of that hope, and he loved the looks of it. He was back there the next Sunday and the next and the next. He always got there late. He always left early. Did not want any attention.

On about the sixth or seventh Sunday, the message was so moving, so powerful, so encouraging that he forgot all about the time. He did not even notice that there were people who had come in and sat down behind him. Suddenly, the message appeared to him as if there were an overhead looking right at him. It said, "For you, little Ben Hooper of unknown heritage, there is hope in the future." He got so carried away with it that he forgot about everything, and suddenly the message was over.

He stood up, expecting to run out again as he had in weeks past, but this time the aisles were clogged, and he couldn't get through. As he was trying, he felt a hand on his shoulder. He turned, looked around, and looked up. He was looking right into the eyes of the young pastor, who asked him a question which had been on the minds of everybody there for the last twelve years: "Whose boy are you?"

Instantly the church grew deathly quiet. Slowly a smile started to come across the face of the young minister until it broke into a huge grin. Then he said,

"Oh, I know whose boy you are. The family resemblance is unmistakable. You are a child of God."

With that, he swatted him across the rear and said, "That's quite an inheritance you got there, boy. Now go and see to it that you live up to it." Many years later, little Ben Hooper said that that was the day he was elected governor of the State of Tennessee, and later reelected.

To be candid, I lost my earthly father when I was five years old. I met my heavenly father when I was forty-five years old. I don't remember my earthly father. I can never forget my heavenly father. When I became a child of the King, that's when everything changed. I started looking at biblical truths about success, and I checked them out psychologically and theologically, because a lot of people want to have all the bases touched.

At age forty-five, I was stone broke and in debt. I'd been working hard all of my life. I've always been optimistic. I'd go after Moby Dick in a rowboat and take the tartar sauce with me. That's my basic nature.

But nothing really happened until I looked at just who I was. That's why I keep saying, you have to *be* before you can *do*; you have to *do* before you can *have*. Failure is an event; it's not a person. Yesterday really did end last night. Today is a brand new day, and the day is yours.

Now as went you went down the above list, did you put down most of those as being attitudes? Or did you put down that most of them were skills?

The reality, ladies and gentlemen, is the best news I can possibly give you: they are all skills. Let me tell you why that's so critically important. It means they can be taught. If they can be taught, that means you can learn them.

If our kids were taught those things in our schools, do you believe that we would have a reduction in drug usage, violence, teenage pregnancy, and all of those things?

There's one exception. We cannot teach faith in our schools anymore. We did for the first 200 years; we just can't do it anymore. You ever seen a New England primer that was used for 200 years in America? You know how they taught the alphabet? A, and a Bible verse. B, and a Bible verse. C, and a Bible verse. That's the way they taught it.

Ever pick up one of McGuffey's *Readers*? You know what they were talking about? You got it, but we can't use that anymore. As a matter of fact, you'll get in less trouble taking God's name in vain than taking it in praise. Tragic, but that happens to be the way it is.

If all of these other qualities were taught, would we have better students? Would we be able to cut all those other things down? I can tell you empathically we know it will, because our company has a program that teaches how to develop these qualities there. And yes, drug use does come down. Yes, teenage pregnancy does come down. Yes, grades do go up. Yes, attendance is better, because these are qualities that really will make a difference.

Would you love to have a mate with all of those qualities? Do wish your kids had all of these qualities? Do you wish your boss had those qualities? How about your employees? Would you wish they had those qualities? Do you wish that all teachers had them? And all the politicians?

How about your doctor and your lawyer—what if they had all of those qualities? Would we have a better world?

Now let me ask you a question. How many of you when you were in school had a course which taught you how to develop all of these qualities? Let me also ask, do you believe that we're missing the boat in education?

Boy, isn't that a relief? All this time you thought that it was your fault that you haven't done more with your life, and now we have identified what the culprit is. It's those educators. Boy, I can't wait until tomorrow. I'm going to get on the telephone. I'm going to call them, and I'm going to tell them a thing or two, you bet I am. I'm going to be teaching some stuff like this.

Before you get too exercised about it, let me ask you some questions. How many hours a day do kids go to school? Let's say they go seven hours a day. How many days a year do they go to school? One hundred and eighty. That means they're in school 1,260 hours a year, or roughly 65 percent of that time, they're in class learning things.

Now how many hours are there in a year? There are 8,760 hours. The kids actually are in school 1,260 hours a year, they're at home 7,500 hours a year, and mom and dad had the kids 40,000 hours before the teacher ever saw them.

With that in mind, do you think mom and dad should assume some of the responsibility for teaching these qualities and values? Do you believe that it would be ideal if mom and dad taught these qualities, the teachers reinforced them, and then the business community implemented them?

Are you beginning to understand now why I talk about your personal life, your family life, and your business life all together? They go together, don't they?

Another question. Do you believe that it would be helpful if the parents and the teacher and the business community acquired some of those qualities before they started teaching them? What do you call a person that practices one thing and preaches another? A hypocrite.

As you well know, a hypocrite is a fellow who gripes and complains about the sex, nudity, and violence on his VCR. A hypocrite is simply a fellow who is not himself on Sunday. I get so amused that every once in a while somebody will say, "I don't go to church. Nothing but a bunch of hypocrites down there." I always say, "Friend, don't let that stop you. Come on down. We got room for one more. Not only that, but if a hypocrite is standing between you and God, that just means the hypocrite's a little closer to God than you are."

Anyhow, when you put these things together, if they were taught at home, reinforced in school, and implemented in the business community, then we really would have a going Jesse, as we would say at home.

Do you believe that if these were taught, it would helpful in getting a job anywhere at any time under any circumstances, improving our employment security? Would it help a person to be a better doctor, a better lawyer, a better mechanic, a better teacher, a better anything?

Now suppose a doctor had every one of these skills. Would you still want him to go to medical school and learn something about medicine? If your mechanic had every one of these skills, would you also want him to know how to fix a car?

In other words, whatever you do, you have to have the specific skill for it. But this will give you the base to build on. Regardless of the profession you choose, I can teach anybody how to run the gizmo that manufactures the widgets. We can teach them procedure, and that's what the employers tell me everywhere: you send me somebody with these qualities; I'll teach him the others.

They say, "Yes, but Zig, those are values." They sure are. So are lying, cheating, stealing, and irresponsibility. If you don't teach one set, guess what's going to happen. They will acquire the others with very little effort on their part.

Very few parents have cussing sessions, where they get the kids together and say, "OK, kids, tonight we're going to learn three of the filthiest words you have ever heard." They don't do those kind of things, but they pick them up from society, from television, from the radio. Hey, they're going to learn it anyhow.

This is really all about the importance of being consistent. I think Nathaniel Hawthorne said it best: "You cannot be one kind of person long and another kind of performer and get by with it. You ultimately become confused as to who you are, and your effectiveness is dramatically reduced."

A lot of people say, "Zig, aren't kids basically good?" Anybody who asks that question has never watched a two-year-old deal with a new baby brother. I can absolutely guarantee: no, they are not basically good. We have to teach them to be good.

I love the story of the old Eskimo. Many years ago, in northern Alaska, they used to have dogfights every Saturday. They were vicious. This old Eskimo owned two dogs, a black one and a white one, and they would always put on an incredible fight. They almost killed each other every Saturday, and after a period of time they'd finally beaten themselves up so badly they couldn't fight anymore. The Eskimo retired them.

One Saturday somebody asked him, "You know, I noticed something rather interesting. I noticed that invariably when you bet on the black dog, the black dog won. When you bet on the white dog, the white dog won. How on earth could you tell?" The old Eskimo kind of smiled and said, "It's pretty easy. I just always bet on the one I'd been feeding all week."

I bet on the individual who feeds the best part of their nature with the good, the clean, the pure, the powerful, and the positive. That's the individual that I'm going to bet on over a period of time.

What are we feeding our young people today? The typical eighteen-year-old has watched 17,000 hours of television, has listened to 11,000 hours of music, has watched 2,000 hours of MTV or movies. This does not count telephone time. It does not count athletic-event attendance. It does not count dating. It does not count riding around.

In 30,000 hours, you can send your child through kindergarten, grade school, high school, college, medical school, and have them serve an internship and a fellowship. It seems to me that's a better use of the time.

So the kids have had 30,000 hours of being directly entertained, and yet when you're around the house with them, the one thing you hear the most is "I'm bored."

Interesting, isn't it? You can't entertain people for life. At some point, we have to wean them and start teaching them responsibility. We have to start teaching them that they have some things they absolutely must do. They have to learn on their own.

Don't misunderstand. I believe there should be some pleasure in life. I believe that if you don't have some pleasure, you're not going to end up being very happy. You have to have pleasure, but we ought to always ask ourselves three questions about pleasure.

Number one, can I repeat this pleasure indefinitely and be happy? Some pleasures you cannot repeat indefinitely and be happy. They tell me that the first time a person deals with coke, there's a pleasurable sensation that absolutely defies belief. It is absolute ecstasy. That's what those who've done it say.

The second thing they say is that never again do they ever hit that same emotional high, that feeling of ecstasy as they did on that very first trip, although they will continue to try. Then something rather fascinating happens, frightening really. The coke destroys the brain's ability to reproduce dopamine and norepinephrine, and without those two neurotransmitters, it is impossible to experience joy and happiness.

They sought a shortcut to happiness, but through that pleasure destroyed any chance of being happy. Can I repeat this pleasure indefinitely without any danger?

Number two, is it morally right and fair to everyone concerned? You cannot be happy on somebody else's back. It just does not work that way. If you've taken from somebody, you're going to have a very short-term pleasure; permanent happiness is not going to be there.

Number three is kind of hitting you below the belt: would I be willing for my mama to know I'm doing this? To put it another way, would I be willing for this to show up in tomorrow morning's headlines?

We need to teach responsibility, but here's the exciting thing, and I think it's tremendously exciting: what you do *off* the job determines how far you go *on* the job. It also determines how well the kids do in school.

As I said, they did a study on the typical American factory. The person who works by the hour on the line watches an average of thirty hours of television a week. The person in charge of the line watches an average of twenty-five hours of television a week. The foreman watches twenty hours. Are you noticing a little trend there?

The plant superintendent watches twelve to fifteen hours of television a week. The president watches eight to twelve hours. The chairman of the board watches four to eight hours, and 50 percent of that time he or she is watching a training video.

One publication recently came out with this data about how 47 percent of the people feel they never have time to do anything, and yet the same people are saying they spend endless, mindless hours watching television, and two days later they don't have a clue as to what they learned.

Here's my question. Those people who work on the line by the hour watching thirty hours of television a week—do you believe that if they were to take ten of those hours and get involved in personal growth and development and seminars and reading and learning and study they might not have permanent jobs working by the hour on the line? Does that make any sense at all, folks?

I don't think there's any question about it. In other words, we are not victims. There are some things that we can do to take responsibility and to take action.

Do we really need to teach our kids all of these qualities? Well, let me give you this information. The Search Institute out of Minneapolis, Minnesota did a survey of 270,000 young people in 600 communities in 33 states. They said, "Our research reveals that 75 percent of American teenagers have 20 or fewer essential developmental assets, the values and standards, the activities and structure that serve both as a safety net against destructive behavior and as an encouragement to positive action."

We're not teaching what they need to know. You give me kids that have been taught these values we've been talking about, these qualities, and I'll give you a kid who's potentially a brilliant producer, who will succeed wherever they are.

USA Today of August 2, 1995 said 70 percent of college students admitted cheating; 29–35 percent of the medical students admit that they had exaggerated on their applications concerning their research; 46 percent of the teens believe lying is OK. The most frightening thing that I think I've ever read in a news article says *only* 31 percent of the adults do.

What do we teach? How do we teach it? The telephone rings in a lot of homes. All the time the parents have been saying "Tell the truth." The telephone rings. "Tell him I'm not home."

Obey the law, but I use a fuzzbuster. What they're really saying is, "Look, kid, if you're going to break the law, don't be a dumb bunny and get caught. Be smart like your old man."

In his book *Corporate Bigamy: How to Resolve the Conflict between Career and Family*, Mortimer Feinberg interviewed a hundred of the CEOs of the Fortune 500 companies and asked them what is necessary to go to the top and stay there. The answer was that they have to build their careers on honesty, character, and integrity. They said that anybody who thinks they can go to the top and stay there who's not honest is dumb. That's about as strong as it can get.

The Josephson Institute of Ethics says an unprecedented proportion of today's youth lack commitment to core moral values like honesty, personal responsibility, respect for others, and civic duty. I'm really not blaming the kids, by any stretch of imagination. It is not the kids' fault. Very few of them own television stations or music stations, and very few of them publish *Penthouse* and *Playboy* and all of that kind of stuff. It's our responsibility civically because, you see, we're all involved in crime and drugs and alcohol.

My son lost his best friend when a drunken teenager ran through a light and killed him at ninety miles an hour. Drugs were involved. My brother-in-law had his home broken into. An heirloom picture was stolen. Two hours later, it was in the veins of the heroin addict who stole it.

I'm involved in crime. I pull up to a service station. It's not as true today as it was, because they have all the automatic stuff out there, but the sign says, "Please pay before pumping." You have to go inside in order to get it.

Here's what psychiatrist Max Levine says. "There cannot be emotional health in the absence of high moral standards and a sense of social responsibility."

It all goes together. There's some good news that goes along with all of this: you already have every single one of the qualities we've identified.

"Ziglar, are you serious? I have all of them? Man, you have to be kidding me. If I had all those qualities, I wouldn't be listening to you. Hey, I'd be up there making the talk, and you'd be listening to me."

Let's look at the first one, which is honesty. Are you going to tell me there's not an honest bone in your body, that you're so crooked that when you die they're going to have to screw you into the ground?

As you go down the list, you will discover that you have the seed of every one of them. You're terribly, terribly weak in many of them. All of us are. That's the reason repetition is so important.

It's the story of the Chinese bamboo tree. They plant the seed, they water it, and they fertilize it, and nothing happens the first year. The second year, they water it, and they fertilize it, and nothing happens. The third year, they water it, and they fertilize it, and nothing happens. The fourth year, they water it, and they fertilize it, and nothing happens. The fifth year, they water, and they fertilize it, and some time during the course of the fifth year, in a period of approximately six weeks, the Chinese bamboo trees grows ninety feet or thereabouts.

Did it grow ninety feet in six weeks, or was it in five years? Think about it for a moment. You know it was ninety feet in five years, because had there been any year when they did not water it and fertilize it, there would have been no Chinese bamboo tree.

In 1952, I dreamed the dream that I'm living right now—that someday I'd be a speaker. It took sixteen years doing it part-time before I was able to do it full-time.

It wasn't until I was forty-five years old that it absolutely exploded. Twenty years I had the dream of a daily newspaper column; I'd pursued every course I knew. Finally I said the right things to the right lady at a seminar in Chicago, Illinois, and a few months later, the syndicated column was launched.

I am simply saying that like the Chinese bamboo tree, there has to be persistence involved. That's one of the qualities. For sixteen years, I struggled desperately to get speaking engagements. For the last twenty-three years I have not solicited a single engagement, and I have to turn more down than I can accept.

One of the reasons, I believe, is that I've hung in there. You know what I do before every seminar, even if I've done it 300, 400, or 500 times? I always invest at least three hours. Because this was a recording, I invested something like twenty hours in getting ready for it. That's on top of reading at other times.

It is not easy, but if you're willing to do these things and organize your schedule, then you can take the time to do the other things that you want to do. Hard work is part of the picture.

Let me tell you why I'm so excited that these things that we've been talking about are skills. You see, since they're skills, they can be taught, they can be learned. That means I have a chance. That means you have a chance. It means that youngster who left the slums this morning without a bite of food to eat, maybe with a kick in the rear, he or she has a chance, if somewhere along the way he or she is fortunate enough to meet a Jaime Escalante.

Some of you will recognize the name and the movie *Stand and Deliver*. An immigrant from Bolivia was teaching in the barrio in Los Angeles, a Mexican community. Drug usage was rampant out there. Crime was high. Teenage pregnancy was bad. A lot of the kids graduated without having an education.

Escalante comes along, and of all things, he said, "I want to teach these kids advanced calculus."

Vision, dream, something big, something worthy. The authorities thought he was crazy. He persisted, and two years later they let him start teaching despite the fact they were saying, "Escalante, these kids have trouble with the multiplication table, and you want to teach them advanced calculus? There's no way."

Three years later, eighteen of his kids took an examination to win a college scholarship. The examination is so difficult to pass that fewer than 2 percent of the seniors in America will even attempt it, but eighteen of his kids attempted it, and eighteen of his kids passed it; seven of them had the highest possible score.

The authorities knew something was wrong: The kids had to cheat. Nobody does this. Oh, they were furious at Garfield High. They were so mad that they wanted them to take the test over. Two of the eighteen accepted other offers—one of them took another college scholarship; another one decided to go in the service. The other sixteen retook it. Every one of them made exactly the same grades they had made the first go-around, and seven years later, fourteen of those sixteen were professionals.

It doesn't make any difference where you start. It's who you are and where you go. The neat thing is these are skills that can definitely be taught. You see, Escalante had given them hope.

I'm going to tell you something, and I tell you with absolute certainly that if you will do it, in one week's time, you'll be able to tell a difference. In two weeks' time, your family will be able to tell the difference. In three weeks' time, anybody who knows you will be able to tell the difference. I'm going to talk to you about talking to yourself. Self-talk.

We have a three-day seminar called "Born to Win." People come from all over the world. Last April 12, I got a letter from a gentleman who is a psychiatrist, Dr. Louis Cady. He's also a concert pianist. He is the one who gave me some counsel in my book *Over the Top*.

Here's what he said in the letter: "The experience of 'Born to Win'" was one of a lifetime, and I have already started putting numerous ideas to work. You also 'sold me' finally, despite my thick skull on using the affirmation card. The results thus far: five days have been almost frightening in their intensity and speed, but in a frighteningly good way."

I'm going to tell you: this will work, it has worked, is working, and will continue to work in my life. It will work in your life. I'm going to encourage you tonight when you get home, to get in front of a mirror. You square your shoulders, you look yourself right in the eye, and if you have a cassette recorder, record it as you go.

You get there, and you say this:

I, Jane Jones, am an honest, intelligent, organized, responsible, committed, teachable person who is sober, loyal, and clearly understands that regardless of who signs my paycheck, I am self-employed. I am an optimistic, punctual, enthusiastic, goal-setting, smart-working, self-starter who is a disciplined, focused, dependable, persistent, positive thinker.

I am an energetic team player who appreciates the opportunity my company and the free-enterprise system offers me. I am thrifty with the company's resources and apply common sense to my daily tasks. I take honest pride in my competence and appearance and am motivated to be and do my best so that my healthy self-image will remain on solid ground. These are the qualities which enable me to manage myself and help give me employment security in a no-job-security world.

Now, folks, I don't read minds. Neither does anybody else, but as you're reading, I'm going to tell you what's probably on your mind right now: "Well, now, Zig, that's a little much. You expect me to make all of those claims. Why, Zig, even if I have the seeds, those seeds are awfully small and awfully weak. I'm so weak in most of them, Zig, How can I honestly do that?"

You can honestly do it because in the book of Joel in the Old Testament, the third chapter, the tenth verse, says this: "Let the weak say, I am strong."

A couple of years ago, I was in Las Vegas. A lady came up to me, and she said, "Mr. Ziglar, I have three daughters. Two of them are honor students, every year. My other one also went to school. She was so overwhelmed by the older two that she just knew she didn't have a chance, and she bought this philosophy that you're talking about right now. She bought this qualities of success idea. She bought the idea of looking herself in the mirror and claiming these qualities. Mr. Ziglar, I'm here to tell you that last year, by a minute fraction of a point, she beat both of her older sisters."

Am I saying this makes you smarter? Absolutely not, but I want you to notice what the qualities are. *I'm honest and intelligent, and I'm a hard worker.* As she started claiming these, she started seeing herself in that light. She started visualizing. She started thinking better. She started working harder, and then, yes, she released what was there.

At the turn of the century, down in Beaumont, Texas, a man bought some property. The oil companies came to him and said, "We believe we have oil there. Let us drill for it. If we hit it, we'll pay you royalties." He had nothing to lose, everything to gain, so they started drilling. The oil well came in, and the first year it had pumped out 18 million barrels out of that field. It was Spindletop, the most productive single oil field in history.

The man became an instant millionaire—or did he? You see, he'd been a millionaire ever since he'd acquired the property, but really until the oil was discovered and brought forth, it had no value. Until you recognize, confess, and develop the qualities you have, you might as well not have them.

The person that won't read is no better off than the person who can't read. The person who won't use the qualities they have is no better off than a person who doesn't have the qualities.

I'm going to give you a couple of other little stories because I think they're so significant. In October of '92, I was in Birmingham, Alabama, doing a public seminar. A gentleman came up to me, and he said, "Mr. Ziglar, I was in Montgomery three years ago when you gave this qualities of success talk." He said, "You didn't put the card in the tapes in those days, so I put my own. I have this 5 x 7 card here," and he pulled it out, and it was pretty dog-eared.

He said, "Every morning and every evening for the last three years, I have claimed these qualities." I said, "Tell me what's happened." He said, "Number one, my income is up over 500 percent. Last year alone, over 300 percent." He sells real estate. Do I need to tell you what the real-estate market was in 1990, 1991, and 1992?

"Let me tell you something else," he said. "Every other facet of my life is dramatically better. My relationship with my family is so much better."

One of the qualities that we put up there is *I am punctual*. He said, "When I read that one, I thought it was the funniest thing I'd ever read in my life, because I've never been on time for anything. I was late more times for school than any kid who ever graduated from the high school in Montgomery. I was late for breakfast, lunch, and dinner. I was late for church, appointments, golf games. I was late for everything. As a matter of fact, the joke was, if you want to have lunch with him at 12:00, tell him it's 11:30, and then he'll be there by 12:00.

"I'd only been doing this a few days when I realized that that was a choice, that I didn't have to be late. I could choose to be there on time. Mr. Ziglar, I haven't been late for anything in over three years, and you'd be amazed at how much better I get along with my friends and family as a result of it." There's no question about the effectiveness of what we are talking about.

The second paragraph. *I, John Jones, am a compassionate, respectful, encourager who is a considerate, generous, gentle, patient, caring, sensitive, personable, attentive, fun-loving person. I am a supporting, giving and forgiving, clean, kind, unselfish, affectionate, loving, family-oriented human being, and I am a sincere and open-minded, good listener, and good-finder who is trustworthy. These are the qualities which enable me to build good relationships with my associates, neighbors, mate, and family.*

Again, Joyce Brothers says you cannot consistently perform in a manner which is inconsistent with the way you see yourself. When you claim to be kind and gentle and loving and affectionate and caring, and then chew your wife or your husband out in a restaurant or somewhere, the minute you do that, your conscience will be pricked, and you'll say, "Hey, that is not me." You will change the behavior.

I'm talking about something that is psychologically and theologically sound, folks, something that will make a difference in your life. There's no question about it. Every day, you do this, morning and night. *I'm a person of integrity with the faith and wisdom to know what I should do and the courage and convictions to follow through.*

I have the vision to manage myself and to lead others. I'm authoritative, confident, and humbly grateful for the opportunity life offers me. I am fair, flexible, resourceful, creative, knowledgeable, decisive, and an extra-miler with a service attitude who communicates well with others. I am a consistent, pragmatic teacher with character and a finely-tuned sense of humor.

I am an honorable person and am balanced in my personal, family, and business life, and have a passion for being, doing, and learning more today so I can be and do more tomorrow.

Then you wind it up. *These are the qualities of the winner I was born to be. Tonight I'm going to sleep wonderfully well. I will dream powerful and positive dreams. Tomorrow I will awaken refreshed, and it's going to be an absolutely magnificent day.*

You will sleep better, and you will dream better dreams, and you will awaken refreshed. It ought to be the last thing you put in your mind at night. That's what the mind is going to be dreaming about and dwelling on and developing. Your creativity goes up. The next morning, you start today with exactly the same procedure. You do that every day for thirty days.

Let me tell you another story. A couple of years ago, I spoke in Los Angeles on a Tuesday morning. Thursday afternoon, my executive assistant, Laurie Majors, got a telephone call from a young man out there.

"Laurie," he said, "I was there Tuesday morning. I bought the set of tapes. I got the card. I've been claiming these qualities every morning and every night. When I claimed them Tuesday night, I was doing good until I got to the word *integrity*, and it bothered me. The next morning, when I got to the word *integrity*, it bothered me again. Wednesday night, it bothered me so badly when I claimed to be a man of integrity, I could not sleep. This morning, when I read it again, Laurie, I knew I had to call you and tell you something. You see, Laurie, I bought the set of tapes and paid for them, this whole 'How to Stay Motivated' series.

"When I got back home, there in the bottom of my bag were the videotapes 'Developing the Qualities of Success.' I hadn't paid for them, and I'm embarrassed about it. I'm calling to tell you I want to pay for them."

Laurie said, "Don't be embarrassed about it. Accidents happen to everybody."

Long pause. "Laurie, it was not an accident. When nobody was looking, I put them in the bottom of my bag."

Folks, the eyes are the windows of the soul. You cannot look yourself in the eye and claim one thing and then behave in an entirely different way and not have it get to you.

I'm talking life-changing stuff. That's what this is all about. Do it every day for thirty days. Then at the end of the thirty days, pick the strongest quality you have. Let's say that you are a very good, positive thinker, but let's say that your organization skills can use some help. You take a 3 x 5 card, and you write on it the top quality—*I am tremendously positive in my thinking. I'm getting better organized every day of my life.*

An amazing thing is going to happen. For example, have you ever noticed that when you buy a green Buick, everybody in town all of a sudden starts driving green Buicks?

What's going to happen is, every time you pick up a newspaper or magazine, there's going to be an article about how to get better organized. You'll go into a coffee shop, and the people in the next booth are talking about how to get better organized. You'll even turn on the television, and they're talking about how you get better organized. The company calls a meeting: hey, we're going to have a seminar on how to get better organized.

You're going to become convinced very quickly that there's a conspiracy out there to help you get exactly what you want out of life, and you know what? You'll be right, because when you get right, and you have direction in your life, you're going to be amazed at the number of people who not only will step aside to let you go, but they will give you a boost and make you get there even faster. When your attitude changes, everything about your life is going to change.

Why is it important that these qualities and values be taught not only in our family, but in our companies? According to the United States Chamber of Commerce, between $20 billion and $30 billion worth of merchandise is stolen by employees every year.

Understand that 98 percent of all businesses have fifty people or less, and 50 percent of all bankruptcies are the direct result of employee theft. In addition to that, according to Robert Half International, employees steal between $220 billion and $230 billion worth of time. The same person who would never think of putting a stapler in their briefcase and taking it home thinks nothing about making personal telephone calls or taking their time at work to write a few personal letters or spending an extra twenty minutes in the restroom although they were there just ten minutes ago. They don't think about that as theft, but in reality it dramatically impacts productivity, and that's where we get in a lot of economic trouble.

It obviously takes time and money to train people properly about qualities and other skills, and some companies say to me, "Why is it I train my people and then lose them?" There's one thing worse than training people and losing them, and that's *not* training them and keeping them. We can measure training costs. We cannot measure how much it costs you not to train your people.

All of these things that we're talking about are applicable in so many areas of life. You can use them for weight loss. You can use them for a golf game. You can use them for anything you want to.

One of my goals is to be the world's number-one husband. I asked the redhead, "Sweetheart, if you could identify your dream husband, what qualities would you want him to have?" Over a period of three or four days, here's what she put together. She wants me to be spiritually sound and committed and faithful. You hear a lot about relativity nowadays. She does not want me to be *relatively* faithful. She wants me to be faithful, period.

She wants me to have integrity, respect her, be unselfish, a good father, with sense of humor. I think one reason we get along so well is the fact that I do have a good sense of humor. She has a fabulous sense of humor, although she doesn't tell jokes. She's never told but three since we've been married, and she blew the punch line on two of them.

Sometime back, every night before we turn out the lights, we started spending a moment or two just looking at each other. A couple of years ago, we were on vacation, and we'd been driving a long way that day. We got in bed, and a few seconds later, I turned the light out. She sat straight up in bed, turned the light back on. She said, "You didn't look at me."

I said, "Sweetheart, I did too."

"No, you didn't."

"I promise you, I looked at you."

"OK, how did I look?"

"You're beautiful. You're absolutely gorgeous. Your eyes are just sparkling. You're sexy."

"You did look," she said.

She wants me to be a good listener. Fellows, that's what your wife wants just about most of all— for you to be sensitive, compassionate, ambitious, considerate, generous, affectionate, gentle, patient. She wants me to have good manners, to be sober, and to be wise.

You know what I do? I put that on my 3 x 5 card, and I regularly look at it, and I ask myself, did I do it today? It's a reminder. We don't need to be told, but we do need to be reminded of how you accomplish those things. Bottom line is, my wife and I are more in love today than we've ever been, because I tell folks that if that woman ever leaves me, I guarantee I'm going with her. No question about that.

The question comes up then: "Ziglar, you talk a whole lot about psychological, theological, and physiological. You talked about the things that everybody wants. You want to be happy and healthy and reasonably prosperous and secure, and have friends, peace of mind, and good family relationships. What does the Bible say about those things?"

Let me tell you what I've done. I've adapted the Bible in scriptural self-talk. Because I'm not a theologian, after I did this, I sent it to two of the most respected Bible scholars I know, and I said, "Tell me if I'm right on. If there's any question at all about it, then I want you to tell me, because I do not want to make an error." I don't believe you fool with and alter God's word, but I also believe that many times, we eliminate many things because we don't clearly understand what God has to say. I've taken several verses on occasion and said, "This is the part I wanted theological validation on," and asked them if this is manipulating the Bible or if it is simply getting from the Bible what the Bible promises.

One of them sent word back to me. He said, "This is now the first page of my book of devotions." I assume by that he's saying it's OK.

In Psalm 84:5, here's what it says: "I am happy because I am strong in the Lord and want above all else to follow His steps."

Proverbs 3:5, 7–8: "I trust and reverence the Lord and turn my back on evil, so He directs me, gives me success, and gives me renewed help and vitality."

Proverbs 3:16–22: "My God-given wisdom gives me a long, good life, riches, honor, pleasure, peace, and living energy."

Psalms 63:7–8. "I am secure beneath the protecting shadow of God's wings and His strong right arm."

First Corinthians 2:16, Galatians 5:22, Matthew 7:12: "As a child of God, with the mind of Christ, the fruit of the Holy Spirit, and a follower of the Golden Rule, I have an eternal friend and a host of earthly friends, and marvelous family relationships."

Isaiah 26:3: "I trust you, Lord, and my thoughts often turn to you, so I am in perfect peace."

As I indicated earlier, I lost my oldest daughter on May 13 of this year. The toughest thing any father, parent, or mother is ever called on to go through. Though the grief is intense and the tears are many, they're bearable simply because we have that peace that passes all understanding. We know where she is, and equally I know that we will see her again.

Psalms 24:14: "I enjoy becoming wise, so there's hope for me, and a bright future lies ahead for me."

Again, failure is an event. It is not a person. I believe with all my heart at this moment you have the keys to a much greater and brighter future. I believe with all my heart that if you will claim and develop these qualities and develop the specific skills your job or profession demands, that I really will see you—and yes, I really do mean *you*—not just at the top. Hey, I'm going to see you over the top. Thank you, and God bless you.

CHAPTER 5

Relationships and Motivation

By now you probably are more alert to a lot of things around you, but let me give you a little test.

Do you wear a wristwatch? Have you had that wristwatch at least a year?

Now please don't look at the watch now, but if you've had it a year, you've looked at it a whole lot of times. The average person looks at their watch about a hundred times a day. (That counts the last ten minutes before lunch and the last ten minutes before they get off.) You ought to know what's on it.

Now don't look at your watch, but I want you to answer these questions to yourself.

First of all, what kind of watch do you have?

Second, does that wristwatch have roman numerals or regular numerals, or does it have numerals at all? Are there blanks or slashes or digits or whatever?

What is straight up and down at the 12:00 slot? What's at the 3:00 slot? Get a picture in your mind. What's at the 6:00 slot, and what's at the 9:00 slot?

Now that you have carefully thought it through, I want you, maybe for the first time since you've owned the watch, to very carefully look at it.

Am I right to assume that you missed at least one of the questions?

I just said I want you to look very carefully at your watch. Do you remember me saying that? OK, what time is it?

The reality is, we don't really look. We don't really listen. We don't really hear. That's the reason you will hear some things that bear repeating over and over.

Now we're going to talk about relationships, because relationships have a direct bearing on your motivation and your attitude in life. How important are they? I love the story of the little guy that interrupted his dad, who was busy at home working. He tried to get his attention, and his dad kind of resisted, and finally the little boy said, "Dad, who do you like best, Batman or Superman?"

The dad said, "I don't know, son."

The boy said, "Oh, come on, Daddy. You like one of them best. Which one do you like the best?"

"OK, I like Superman the best."

The little boy said, "OK," and he looked at his dad and said, "Aren't you going to ask who I like best, Daddy?"

The dad said, "All right. Who do you like best?"

"I like Batman."

"Why do you like Batman?"

"Batman has a friend."

Isn't that's what all of us really want? Aren't our relationships so enormously important? Yet a lot of times we seem to move them to the back burner. They're not in our minds. They're something that can wait for nurturing and developing.

We get wrong information from time to time. When I was a young speaker, I heard a well-known speaker, a philosopher, say that you're where you are in life because that's really where you want to be. I've always liked to sound philosophical, so I started telling people that you're where you are because that's where you want to be.

One night, I was in Birmingham, Alabama, on my way to Meridian, Mississippi. It was very important that I be there, because I had an engagement the next morning.

The roads were under repair. I stopped and asked a service-station attendant, "How do you get from here to there?" A very kind young man. He not only told me how to get there but drew me a little map. He said, "You follow this map, and it'll take you right on into Meridian."

An hour later, I saw another sign, and it revealed that I was now forty-five miles further from Meridian than I had been when I asked for the directions. I can absolutely assure you that I was not there because that's where I wanted to be. I wanted to be closer to Meridian. I was there because a well-intentioned individual had given me wrong directions.

I would suggest that if you're broken and dead and not getting along well with the people that are important to you, you're not where you want to be. You could be there because over a period of time, you have followed some wrong directions.

A lot of people ask, "Do I really have what it takes to be successful in what I want to do? Do I have the qualities necessary?"

I want to use a little analogy to get you to thinking along these lines. Let's say that you have it made financially. You've socked away quite a bit of money, so you want to build your dream house. You go to the architect and say, "I want you to design me the most beautiful plans you can possibly do." He is a world-renowned architect, and he puts the plans together. They are absolutely magnificent.

Then the architect goes to the best builder in town, who has the best reputation, and says to him, "We want you to follow these plans exactly. Use the best materials, use the best laborers, get the best carpenters, brick masons, laborers, electricians, plumbers, the very best materials, all of it."

Finally the house is complete. You move in, have a big party. The landscaping is absolutely gorgeous. You just know you are going to have a long, happy life there, but about three months later, little cracks start to appear in the walls. Six months later, the city comes in and inspects it and says, "You have to move out. We condemned the house."

Who is at fault? Is it the builder, or is it the architect? As you think on this, you clearly understand it has to be the architect. The builder followed the directions precisely, used the best materials, used the laborers. The plan was faulty.

Is there a possibility that you have everything that you need to be enormously successful, but simply have not developed it? Or that you've been listening to the wrong plans along the way? If you have the wrong plans, the wrong direction, I don't care how many positive qualities you have, you're going to end up in the wrong place.

I want to emphasize something, and you've heard me say it already several times. Failure is an event. It is not a person. Yes, today really did end last night. Today is a brand new day.

A lot of times people do not start well, but they end well. A British pediatrician named Illingworth points out that Yeats and Shaw were both poor spellers. Franklin, Adler, and Jung were poor mathematicians. Poe, Shelley, and Whistler were all expelled from school. Edison at age nine was asked to leave because he was at the bottom of the class. Gauguin was labeled a dreamer. Watt was declared dull and inept, and Einstein as mentally slow. You see, a lot of times what people do initially can be corrected. Failure really is an event.

Now as we work on attitudes and relationships, let me ask you a question. Now, I am sixty-nine years old.

Am I old or young? Before you answer the question, let me ask you the next question. Do you have any confidence in what Webster's dictionary has to say?

Well, he's an authority in my life, so I went to Webster, and I looked up what *old* and *young* were. *Old* is someone who has outgrown their youthfulness, belonging to the past, shabby, stale. Now am I old or young? More importantly, are *you* old or young? It has nothing to do, really, with your birthdays. *Young* is described by Webster to be youthfully fresh in body or mind or feeling. Significant, is it not?

I'm really talking about an attitude, not just about relationships, but about life, about your job, about every facet of life itself. I love what Dr. Smiley Blanton says: "I have never seen a single case of senility in people, no matter how old as long, as they maintain an active interest in other human beings and in things outside of themselves."

By now, you know that I do validate things psychologically, theologically, and physiologically before I verbalize it, write it, or record it. I happened to check on this particular thing, and my sources will not go quite that far. I asked whether it would be accurate to say that Alzheimer's is a disease, but senility can be the result of choices we make. They said, yes, that is absolutely on the target.

What are the choices we make? How do we take care of our bodies, our physical, our mental, and our spiritual life? Are we on a growth program? Because all the research I'm doing shows that, provided you remain active physically and mentally, the older you get, the more creative you are. There's no reason whatever for you not to get some marvelous results when you are a senior citizen.

Emerson put it this way. "We don't count a man's years until he has nothing else left to count." If we remain mentally active, if we remain physically active, then those birthdays are not going to be there. As I mentioned earlier, I honestly believe I'm five, maybe ten years away from reaching my peak.

I want to be like old Caleb in the Bible. Caleb was at age eighty-five, and the Lord said, "What part of this real estate do you want?" He said, "Give me the mountaintop where the Philistines are." He said, "I'm feel like I am forty years old. Put me amongst them."

How effective he was, I think, is visibly demonstrated by the fact that there ain't no Philistines around today. He took care of that situation big time.

If we are going accomplish anything, as you've already heard me say half a dozen times, I believe motivation is the key. Motivation does make a difference—motivation towards building a better relationship, a better career, a better family, a better community—the whole ball game is involved there.

There are three kinds of motivation. One is fear motivation. I think fear motivation is best exemplified by the story out of West Texas. If you're not from Texas, you might not know this, but when Texans are rich, they're just richer than anybody. I mean, they really are.

Well, this was a rich Texan. Had about 65,000 acres in his spread, had about 497 producing oil wells, had about 10,000 head of cattle, and he had a magnificent mansion with an Olympic-sized swimming pool. He also had a daughter of marriageable age.

He decided to throw a coming-out party. In sales, we call this *group prospecting*. He invited all of the eligible young men of the area to come. Along about midnight, he took them outside next to the magnificent Olympic-sized swimming pool, which he'd had the foresight to stock with water moccasins and alligators.

He said, "The first one of you young men who will jump into this pool and swim the length of it, I'll give you three choices: $5 million in cash, 1,000 acres of best land, or the hand of my beautiful daughter in marriage. As you know, she is my only heir, so the one who gets her gets the whole deal."

About the time those words came out of his mouth, there was a loud splash at one end of the pool, followed almost immediately by the writhing at the other end of the pool of this dripping young man. The young man climbed out of the pool, the host ran to him, and said, "Son, that's wonderful. You've won. What do you want? Is it the $5 million in cash?"

He said, "No, sir."

"Do you want 1,000 acres of land with all of the oil wells on it, and so forth?"

"No, sir."

"Do you want the hand of my daughter in marriage?"

"No, sir."

"Well, son, what do you want?"

"I want to know the name of that dude that pushed me in the swimming pool." Now that's fear motivation.

Sometimes fear motivation works with small children. For example, you tell a seven-year-old, "If I ever catch you with a cigarette in your mouth, I'm going to wear you out, boy." Now that's fear motivation, and it might have an effect. You tell a fifteen-year-old that, and you're just backing up.

Fear motivation is sometimes effective in an employment situation, where you can temporarily persuade a person that if they don't get there on time from here on in, it is all over. Fear motivation, however, does have its limitations. Where danger is involved, it's a very healthy thing. It's called *fight or flight*.

I don't know how you feel about it. I'd a lot rather people say, "Wow, look how fast he runs" than "Boy, don't he look natural." So the running part of fear is involved.

Then there is *incentive motivation*. We've all seen the picture of the donkey pulling the cart, and the driver has a carrot dangling on a fishing pole right in front of the donkey's mouth. The donkey starts pulling, and he thinks he's going to get a bite of that carrot. Ultimately you have to give him a bit, otherwise the donkey wises up and said, "It's no kind of deal," and so he quits pulling.

He gets a bite of the carrot, then you have another deal. He's no longer hungry, so in order to get him to keep on pulling, you have to shorten the stick, or sweeten the carrots. You have to do something else or lighten that load in order to get him to keep on pulling.

There comes a time in our life when incentive motivation reaches its peak, and we no longer want the bigger house, the bigger car, the second home, and what have you. The type of motivation that I'm going to be talking about is *growth motivation*. Growth motivation really is as you're doing right now: you are learning some things that hopefully will make a difference.

Life itself is kind of like a tire on an automobile. Most of the time when you have tire trouble, it is not a blowout. It's the result of a slow leak: over a period of time, all of the air goes out of the tire, and then all of the sudden one day you say, "Hey, I have a flat here."

I've been talking about self-talk a whole lot as we've gone along in this book, and basically most people are guilty of negative, not positive, self-talk.

I'm so amazed 99.9 percent of all of the golfers who play at a twenty handicap or less will emphasize the importance of the mental aspect of the game. I think golf pro Eldridge Miles would say, "Yes, that really is important." But the overwhelming majority of the golfers, although they say attitude is important, give themselves negative instruction. They miss a ball, and they say, "You dummy, can't you ever do anything right? Idiot, you have to hit the ball straighter. You can't do anything, you dummy."

What does that do to your game? Does it improve your game? When you step up there as an idiot for your next shot, are you really going to be more effective?

The same thing is true regardless of what we're doing. Nate Lipton, my ophthalmologist, is seated here, and when he's examining my eyes, I hope he doesn't ever think along the lines of "Boy, I don't know if I can do this or not. This is a tough one here in front of me." I want him to think as he does, and that's optimistic, positive, and upbeat, and that's what I'm talking about. I want the talk to be a very positive self-talk.

We use negative phrases. For example, we call those electrical appliances on street corners red lights or stop lights or traffic lights, when really their major function is to make traffic go more smoothly, more safely, and more orderly.

A lot of people today say, "I don't have time to do anything." The interesting thing is motivation creates the energy, and direction creates time.

Let me ask you a question. Have you ever had one of those days? You wake up, you go out, and you have a flat tire. You go to change it, but the jack is broken, and the next-door neighbor, who's generally a good person and lets you borrow things like that, is gone. You have to go across the street.

You finally get it, you get down to work, and you notice the office is strangely dark. The electricity has been cut off. You hook up a generator, and you get the phone call saying the administrative assistant is not going to be able to make it. Two hours later, somebody else calls in. One thing after another, all day long. You're really having it tough.

Mercifully, the day ends at 5:00, and so you head home, and you're not whipped, you are whooped. I mean, you've been drove hard and hung out wet. You have had it that day. You walk in, and your wife greets you very enthusiastically. "Oh, honey, I'm so glad you didn't have to work today. Today is the day." You say, "The day for what?"

"Oh, honey, don't tell me you forgot. Today is the day we're going to clean the garage."

"Oh, honey, no, not today."

"Don't worry about it," she says, "it's not going to take us more than two, three, four hours at most. I'll work with you, and we'll get—"

"Honey, I can't put one foot in front of another."

About that time the telephone rings. You struggle over to it, and with the last breath of energy you have, using both hands, you lift the telephone to your ear and say, "Hello." The voice at the other end says, "Hey, partner. I have a tee time at the club in seventeen minutes. We can get in now and fast if you feel like it."

"*If* I feel like it?" Do you know exactly what I'm talking about? All right.

There are a lot of things we don't like to do, like cleaning the garage. How can we deal with that? I have a friend up in Lawton, Oklahoma. Her name is Edna Hennessey. She owns a big beauty parlor, a big beauty school, and what have you. A very upbeat, optimistic, positive, successful lady.

Her mother had been in a nursing home for some little while, and every morning at 10:00, Edna would go see her mother. If somebody called for an appointment to see her at that point, she said, "No, I have to go see Mom at 10:00." Then one day her mother died. Somebody called, and she started to say, "No, I have to go see my mom." Then she said, "Oh, I wish I could get to go see my mom."

It's amazing. It's absolutely astonishing what happens in your attitude when we change the *got-to's* to the *get-to's*.

I'm not talking about being on cloud 87 all the time. I'm not talking about these finger poppers that go around. You wonder if all of them are there, and then you talk to them and realize it's not. I'm not talking about being high all the time. As a matter of fact, people who are high all the time are on something that's going to kill them.

I'm talking about getting to the position where we can do something about our attitude and keep it very positive. The other day I was walking with my middle daughter, Cindy, and we were talking, as we always do, and she said, "You know, Dad, when I first starting using our Performance Planner Plus, I just hated that thing. It was a little cumbersome. I had to carry it with me everywhere I go, and I'd forget it, and I'd leave it, and I'd forget it, and I'd leave it, but you know, Dad, as I started using it and disciplining myself to follow through on it, I'd be absolutely helpless today without it."

She said something very significant: "You know, Dad, every night when I make my list, and the next morning every time I check off a task completed, I feel just a little bit better about myself." Image building, motivating, right there.

After that, I was taking a shower, and as I take a shower, I don't sing. I've been asked not to do that even in showers. I mean, we do have neighbors. Those of you who recognize the name Mitch Miller, if you're old enough for that—he once wrote me a letter asking me not even to bother to sing along with him, if you know what I mean.

I got to thinking that what happens is that the spray of the shower activates a lot of the factors in your skin, and you're physiologically energized. You feel better, and as I was there, getting cleaner, I was thinking, "You know, this will clean me up and lift me up. It's a liquid massage, but it's not permanent."

Sometimes people say, "Is motivation permanent?" No, but neither is bathing. That doesn't mean I have any opposition to bathing. As a matter of fact,

I encourage it. I hope you do, too. I hope you participate, I guess I should say.

Motivation does the same thing to my mind. It
clears my thinking. It generates creativity. It's mentally stimulating. It's emotionally uplifting, though it
is not a permanent thing; it has to be repeated, just like
eating. Wouldn't it be wonderful if our mind growled
when it was beginning to have a difficulty, like our
stomach does when it's running a little bit empty?

Motivation, you see, energizes. It brings on creativity. It makes you friendlier. It makes you more
productive. That has a direct bang on the things
we've been talking out all the way through. That
is, everybody wants to be happy and healthy and at
least reasonably prosperous and secure. They want
to have friends, peace of mind, good family relationships, and hope that the future is going to be better.

Motivation is definitely a contributing factor in
that. You might say, "I don't necessarily love my job."
Again I refer you back to Edna Hennessey: if you
change the expression from got-to to get-to, it'll make
a difference.

A number of years ago, my wife and son and I
were in a steakhouse having dinner, and as we first
sat down, the busboy came along to put the ice water
in for us. This young man splashed the water and ice
out and splashed it out in the second and third one. I
just looked him and said, "Don't like your job, huh?"
He said, "No, I don't." I said, "Well, don't worry about
it. You're not going to have it very long."

I don't know if you ever saw any of those old slap-stick movie comedies where you'd have a waiter, and he's doing something, and something goes astray, and he runs back quickly and disappears in the kitchen. Then he turns around and instantly comes back out. That's what that kid did. He scowled his way in and came out. The kid was grinning so wide it looked like he'd walked through a swinging door on somebody else's push. He was excited, and he came over, and this time he poured the water gently.

He realized that he wasn't going to have that job long with that attitude. Now he *gets to* put the water in the glass instead of *has to* put the water in the glass.

We really do live in a spoiled society. We've been raised to believe that if it doesn't look good, taste good, and smell good, or isn't fun to do, then we really should not have anything to do with it. We want instant gratification in everything, and that's the sign of an immature individual. Patience is one of those qualities we've already talked about as far as success is concerned.

I don't believe there's a human being alive who loves to do what they do as much as I do. I get excited about a lot of things. The redhead says I get excited reading the phone book. Now I don't think that is quite true, but I love what I do, although I don't love to do some of the things that are involved, when I have a five-hour delay, and I'm seated out on the run-way, and the air conditioning in the airplane is not working. I don't get overly motivated about that, but there's nothing I can do about it. So now I can either sit there and shoo and fuss and gripe and complain or I can do what I learned years and years ago to do, and that is to always have something that I can constructively work on when the unexpected happens, so I will always make it a positive instead of a negative experience. It's called *discipline*.

Discipline is a word that people don't care a whole lot about today, but when you discipline yourself to do the things you need to do when you need to do them, the day is going to come when you can do the things you want to do when you want to do them.

Consider this. The sailor only has freedom of the seas when he's absolutely disciplined to be completely obedient to the compass. Until he obeys the compass, he has to stay within sight of the shore, but the moment he trusts the compass and is obedient to it, he can go anywhere in the world the boat will let him go.

Now is the one who is close to the shore because he's not obedient to the compass the one who's free, or is it the one who is obedient to the compass and can go anywhere in the world he want to go? I think the question is self-answering, is it not?

Suppose you're not really in love with the job you do. You can fall in love with the way you do the job, and when you fall in love with the way you do the job, it's just a question of time before you will like certain aspects of the job better. Then one or two things will happen. They will either move you up to a better job, or you will be given a better job somewhere else. The law clearly states that when you do more than you're paid to do, someday you will be paid more for what you do.

For years, *The Boston Globe* carried on its editorial page this wise observation: "I'm an old man, and have had many troubles; most of them never happened."

Expectancy is so important. Robert Updegraff says this: "Be thankful for the troubles of your job. They provide about half your income, because if it were not for the things that go wrong, the difficult people you have to deal with, and the problems and unpleasantness of your working day, someone could be found to handle your job for half of what you're being paid."

It takes intelligence, resourcefulness, patience, tact, and courage to meet the troubles of any day. That is why you hold your present job, and it may be the reason you aren't holding down an even bigger one. If all of us would start to look for more troubles and learn to handle them cheerfully and with good judgment as opportunities rather than irritations, we would find ourselves getting ahead at a surprising rate. It is a fact that there are plenty of big jobs waiting for men and women who aren't afraid of the troubles connected with them.

I *get to* instead of I *got to*. You will learn to love your job, and then you'll get better at the job, and then you'll either get the better job or another opportunity.

Attitude is so important. I love what John Maxwell, a good friend of mine, says: "Never underestimate the power of your attitude. It is the advancement of our true selves. Its roots are inward but its fruit is outward. It is our best friend or our worst enemy. It is more honest and more consistent than our words. It has an outward look based on past experiences. It is a thing which draws people to us or repels them. It is never content until it is expressed. It is the librarian of our past, it is the speaker of our present, and it's the profit of our future."

I'm suggesting a change in thinking, am I not? There's an old saying: if you keep on doing what you've been doing, you're going to keep on getting what you've been getting. If you like what you've been getting, that's OK. If you don't like what you've been getting, we better recognize that maybe the reason for it is, we *got* to do things instead of we *get* to do things.

Most people that I talk to would be in denial. They would deny that that's the way they think, and, again, they think denial is just a river in Egypt. They deny that those basic things are there, and so we need to look at it in that relationship or that light.

Now we're going to talk a whole lot about relationship motivation at this point, but here's my observation and the observations of many other people: If you're getting along well with the people you love, almost regardless of how the rest of your life is going, overall you're a pretty happy camper. If you're not getting along with the people you love, regardless of how many bucks you have in the bank, and regardless of your corporate position, overall you simply are not a very happy camper. Those relationships are enormously important.

My friends who are in counseling in the church and in psychology and psychiatry tell me that nearly 100 percent of the counseling they do is a direct result of relationship problems. Husband, wife, parent, child, employer, employee, teacher, student, brother, sister. Why is that? Why do we have so much relationship difficulty?

I think the major problem started maybe forty years ago, when as a nation, as a people, we started adopting a hooray-for-me, to-heck-with-you attitude: I'm going to do it my way, if I have to win through intimidation; I'm going to look out for number one. I just described the most miserable human being imaginable.

I challenge you to show me one happy person who is self-centered. Invariably, when your thoughts are on yourself, you're not a happy, productive, individual.

A number of years ago, I was bowling in Omaha, Nebraska, and injured my right knee. One of my friends, who is not overly bright, to be kind to him, mentioned something about age. That's where his lack of brightness shows, because you see, there was nothing at all wrong with my left knee. So age obviously had nothing whatever to do with it.

Anyhow, I injured my right knee. That evening I was to speak, and as I came hobbling out, I could just feel the audience say, "Well, look at old Zig. Bless his heart. He's all crippled up, but I bet he's going to do the best he can. I know he's going—" Oh, I could just feel it in the audience.

They had a microphone with a cord on it. I hung the microphone around my neck. To this day, I do not clearly understand what having a microphone around your neck does to your knee, but was an instant healing. I mean that sucker quit hurting right then and there, and for the next sixty minutes, I was up and down and around about, stooping, squatting, shouting, hooting.

At the end of the sixty minutes, they took the mic off my neck, and I stepped off the platform and collapsed. Literally. Now what happened? For sixty minutes, I wasn't thinking about Zig. I was thinking about the audience. I don't remember doing this consciously, but apparently when I stepped off the platform, I was thinking, "OK, Zig, man now think about yourself," and boom. Down I went.

I can guarantee that people who are completely self-centered are miserable human beings. The basic problem is, we do live in that self-centered, selfish world, yet what we do with our life is so dependent on other people.

In my office, I have what I call my Wall of Gratitude. There are nineteen people there who've had a substantial influence on my life. I wonder where I would be had it not been for those nineteen people. You show me anybody in life who's done anything at all, and I will show you somebody who's had a lot of help getting there.

Motivation is important, but there is negative motivation as well as positive. As you will recall, I talked about the fact that when you hear a motivational presentation on success, your brain is flooded with dopamine, norepinephrine, serotonin, and neurotransmitters and so forth, and you're physiologically energized.

Unfortunately, for some people gambling produces the same results. Pornography produces the same results. A lot of times rock music produces the same results, but basically you're energized and activated to go do the wrong thing.

Dr. Forest Tennant—a good friend of mine; I consider him perhaps the number-one brain chemist in America, certainly the number-one drug authority—says if you can put all of those neurotransmitters in there with positive directions on what to do with your life, then you're going to get some marvelous results.

When you listen to things over and over that advise you to abuse a woman or kill a cop or try the suicide solution, over a period of time it definitely is going to have some negative results. Motivation can be negative, but it can also be tremendously and powerfully positive. That's the concept here: to make the motivation powerful, including the directions on how to get the things out of life you really want.

But back to relationship motivation, because it's so important. I want to set up a little scenario which identifies the problem and offers a solution at the same time. It's Friday afternoon in this little scenario. The husband has been out of town all week. It's about 5:00. He gets to the front porch, he's laden with luggage, and he has his briefcase bulging with work he has to do. He doesn't want to set the briefcase and luggage down to ring the doorbell, so he kicks the door.

He doesn't kick it gently—bang, bang, bang. His wife comes to the front door, somewhat startled, and sees him standing there. He doesn't move. He just says, "I've been to a meeting. That's the reason I'm late. I'm glad I went to that meeting, because I learned some things that just bother the hang out of me. I learned that there's some rights around this house that I have not been getting. I have made a list of them, and the first thing you and I are going to do, woman, we're going to sit down, we're going to make some changes around here. You can absolutely count on it."

I can imagine in this scenario that the wife says, "Well, buster, I didn't go to the meeting. I didn't have to go, and I don't have a list written out. I have it burned indelibly into my mind. You bet I want you to come on in, because there are going to be some changes around here. You can count on it. I don't think you're going to like all of them."

Don't you know they had a wonderful, loving, fun-filled weekend? Don't you know that on Monday morning they each awakened raring and ready to go and get out there and turn the world upside down in a very positive way?

Same scenario, same husband, Friday afternoon, 5:00. This time instead of kicking the door down, he gently taps it. His wife comes to the door and he says, "Sweetheart, the reason I'm late is I've been to a meeting, and I'm so glad I was, because I learned some things that troubled me a great deal. I learned that undoubtedly I've not been meeting all of the needs you have. Before we do anything else this weekend, I would like for us to sit down, and I would like for you to share with me how I can become the husband you deserve to have and that you thought you were getting when we got married."

I can well imagine her saying, "Well, it's interesting you mentioned that. I've kind of been thinking about the same thing. Maybe I've not been meeting all of your needs. Let's do sit down and talk about it." Doesn't need any elaboration, does it?

The reality is you really can have everything in life you want if you will just help enough other people get what they want. When you put that other person first, amazing things happen.

Now I don't want to hang a guilt trip on anybody. That's somebody else's department. I'm not talking about the past. I'm talking about the present and using it as preparation for the future. Most of us, when we did what was wrong in the past, we did it based on our circumstances and, more importantly, on the information we had at that time.

As you've heard me say several times, we have to make friends with our past so we can focus on the present in order to make the future what it is capable of being.

I love this particular story about Thomas Carlyle. He was a Scotch essayist and historian who lived from 1795 until 1881. On October 17, 1826, he married his secretary, Jane Welsh. She was a very intelligent person and worked directly with him, but she took ill, and after several years, she had to quit doing the work.

Although Carlyle loved her dearly, he seldom had time to spend with her. He was always busy with his work. Then one day she died. He took her to the cemetery. They buried her. Carlyle came back home. He was sitting in remorse on the side of her bed, and he saw her diary, which was open.

He started reading in it. The first notation he saw: "Yesterday he spent an hour with me, and it was like Heaven. I love him so." He turned the page. "I've listened all day to hear his steps in the hall, but now it is late, and I guess he won't come today."

Carlyle read a little more in the book. Then he threw it down and ran out of the house. Some of his friends found him at the graveside, his face buried in the mud, bitterly weeping tears. For the next fifteen years of his life, he did very little. He was a recluse, nonproductive.

I don't share this with you to hang any guilt trips on anybody. Remember the past is exactly there. I'm talking about planning for the future. We need to invest our time well. Relationships are so incredibly important.

One recent study revealed that of all the things people want in life, 97.8 percent of them said family relationships; better relationships was number one. Then they were asked, how much time do you spend planning to have better relationships? How much time do you set aside for your family? Most of them said, "Well, you know, I'm going to do it. It just seems that I never have time." The most important thing. It doesn't make a whole lot of sense, but that's human nature.

We give in to the urgency of the moment because we do not have a plan. Remember how we talked about how much more we get done on the day before vacation than we do on any other day? Take this same principle, and then plan the time with the family. Plan the time for exercise. Plan the time to get involved in personal growth and development, as you have done.

This philosophy that we're talking about can, among other things, impact racism and sexism. Every quarter at our company, we have what we call the people-builders' meeting. We recognize the outstanding people in our company. We always bring in a corporate client who tells us what our training has meant to them.

We had a lady named Gloria Hogg with Tri-City Hospital, who was our guest speaker on one occasion. It was one of those rainy days: traffic was heavy, she was a little late getting there, and she walked in laughing and smiling and cracking jokes. The trainers who'd been working with her ran up to her, and she grabbed them and hugged them. They kidded a moment, and then Gloria came on, and she kept popping jokes to the group that was there.

Then all of a sudden Gloria came to a dead stop and said, "I don't know if you knew it or not, but you're listening to what was at one time an overtly racist person. If you were not black, I couldn't wait to get on to you and attack you verbally. Being dark brown didn't help. Being yellow didn't help. You had to be black. Otherwise I was after you.

"I've always believed in the Golden Rule," she said, "but I certainly was not living it. As this training started having an impact, saying that you can have everything in life you want if you'll just help enough other people get what they want, I realized that that made nothing but sense. It's nothing new. It's the old Golden Rule handled in a slightly different verbiage. I started going by that thing, and I've never been happier."

For what it's worth, the governor of Texas recognized her as one of the One Hundred Texas Women of Distinction. She had a significant promotion at Tri-City. In addition to that, every morning at 5:30, she gets up and goes out and gives insulin shots, one to a white lady, one to an African-American lady, and one to a Hispanic lady. Once a month, she draws the name of a senior citizen out of a hat and pays that person's electricity bill for the month. She said it gives her a great deal of joy and satisfaction. She said, "Why shouldn't I do it? I have a wonderful job, and a lot of people simply do not have those things."

Does this work? It works because it's intellectually sound. It's psychologically right, and it's the Golden Rule in action. It takes you away from "what's in it for me?" to "what can I do for you?"

A few months later, Elva Gonzales, also at Tri-City, was our guest. When she started with this philosophy, she was a file clerk. Today she heads three departments. Her ten-year-old son was short. He was a runner. He wanted to qualify for this big meet down in Austin. He started training and practicing, and only one person here in the whole Dallas area could qualify. His friends said, "You're too short." She took what she had learned in this approach to life and kept telling him, "If you work hard enough and believe you can, I believe that you can." Bottom line: with thirteen states competing, this youngster finished fourth in the entire thirteen.

From time to time, people say to me, "You changed my life." I'm always flattered when something like that happens, but I have to tell you they have it wrong. I did not change their life. We have some principles and philosophies that are iron-clad. They will work, but it is your choice. Do you put them to work? If you take the philosophy and put it to work, that's what changes your life, not Zig Ziglar, not anybody else. It is what you do. It's a do-it-yourself job.

As you've probably noticed, I get a lot of the heart involved in what I'm talking about. I get you emotionally involved. I used to talk about giving you a checkup from the neck up. I now believe in giving people a checkup from the heart up. I go through the mind because that's the gateway to the heart, but when you change hearts, that's when lives are changed. All change starts with a start. As my friend Joe Sabba says, "You don't have to be great to start, but you have to start to be great."

If relationships are important, how do you get people to like you? In other words, how can you become more likeable? Does it make sense that the more likeable you are, the more friends you'll have, and the better you'll do on the job? Do you believe the boss will promote somebody they like, everything else being equal? Maybe sometimes not even everything else being equal.

Roger Ailes, in an article on personal selling power, says that what others think about you influences what *you* think about you. He said that it only takes another person seven seconds to decide what they really think about you. From that point on, all of their decisions are made largely influenced by that first impression. So that first impression is important.

First impressions are important, and a lot of people start forming impressions before you ever open your mouth. One evening the redhead and I were at our favorite ice-cream parlor. We were having our ice cream, and a young man and his girlfriend walked in. I nudged the redhead, and I said, "Look at that, sweetheart."

"I see him," she said.

"I wonder what happened to him."

"What do you mean?"

"Look at him, he's hurt. He's been in some kind of an accident."

"Oh, honey," she said, "he's not hurt. He's been to the barber shop or the beauty shop."

"Are you trying to tell me that he paid money for somebody to make him look like that?"

"Yes, honey. It happens all the time."

In my lifetime, I have never seen before or since a sight like I witnessed right there. This young man looked like the governor's pardon had gotten to the warden about ten seconds after he plugged in the chair. The hair was all over the place, except there was one piece going straight up, and it must have had two cans of hairspray on it. Had you fallen on it, you would have been hurt. I mean, it was bad. It was green and purple and yellow and orange.

For what it's worth, I would go to war and fight for that young man's right to look exactly like he does. That is America. That's what freedom is all about. You bet I'd fight for his right to look like that, but I wouldn't give him a job.

You know what's so unfortunate about that? He might be absolutely brilliant, extremely well-educated, extremely creative, very, very capable, but with 98 percent of the people in America who have jobs to offer, he'll never get even the interview.

You see, opinion has already been formed, and that opinion influences from there on in. Since likability is important, what are some of the characteristics of the likeable person? Think about it.

I want you to do this. Take three people that you really like. You're attracted to them. What are the things that you really like about them? It probably starts as temporary favorable impressions. The smile the person had would be important, their appearance, as we've talked about. They're friendly, personable, optimistic. Their manners, if they have a sense of humor, if they're good listeners, if they're complimentary, and, now, if they're nonsmokers. Those are things that you automatically notice first off.

Over a permanent basis—integrity, common sense, if they're dependable and loyal and caring and sincere and fair and consistent and committed. In other words, that's not the description of a fair-weather friend. As you know, a fair-weather friend is always there when he needs you. That's not the kind of person that you really want to have a long-term relationship with.

Now the qualities I've just identified are the qualities we've already talked about in this book. By now you recognize that you do have these qualities, and you can use them.

You notice, of course, I'm using emotional words in all of this. When Mark Twain was a cub reporter, he was told by his editor that he must not report anything that he could not validate, that he had not seen, and that he knew for absolute certain was right.

So he went to this occasion, and here's the report he wrote: "A woman giving the name of Mrs. Jane Jones, who is reported to be one of the society leaders of the city, is said to have given what purported to be a party yesterday to a number of alleged ladies. The hostess claims to be the wife of a reputed attorney." When you put that together, it makes you realize that sometimes we can stretch things a little bit too far. What are the advantages, ladies and gentlemen, of being likeable? People who like you generally trust you, and they won't lie to you. They won't deceive you. You can pretty well count on that being true if they really like you.

Number two, they want to do business with you, so they will be more than fair. They want to help you expand your business if they like you. Don't we like to help our friends? They want to do things for you. They might even invite you to play a round of golf with them or go to dinner with them or something. Being the right kind of person is the key.

What's your objective in wanting to be likeable and having all of those friends? As I've said several times, you have to be before you can do. You have to do before you can have, and that is so incredibly important.

Let's look at the motive. Is it motivation, manipulation, or leadership? Motivation is when you try to get somebody to do something for their own good. Manipulation is when you try to get somebody to do something for your own good. Leadership is when you try to get somebody to take an action that will benefit both of you.

Eisenhower said, "Leadership is the ability to persuade somebody else to do what you want them to do because they want to do it." What do they want to do? Things that are in their own best interest. That's what people really want to do.

I saw a young man with a T-shirt on, and the T-shirt said, "I follow no one." I thought, "What a tragedy," because with that kind of an attitude, he will never lead anyone either. You treat people as you see them. This has a direct bearing on the relationship, and the way you treat them influences their opinion of you and how well you get along with them.

My friend Lewis Timberlake from Austin does a lot of speaking. He was invited to speak to a school meeting up in Brooklyn, New York, several years ago. They were honoring a teacher who had been in retirement about ten years. They had had to call her back to assist. They had a class of boys there that, to put it mildly, were slightly out of control. In the first six weeks of school, they had run seven teachers off. It was in desperation that they called her back. They said, "We're going to put a policeman in there so that nothing will happen."

She looked at the list of boys. She said, "You don't have to worry about that. I love to teach boys. I've never had any trouble."

"Yes," they said, "but you've been out of the system for ten years, and there have been some changes made."

She said, "Don't give it a thought. I love boys. I won't have any trouble."

"We'll at least put an assistant in there," they said.

"Hey, I don't need any help at all. I can handle these boys."

It was a marvelous year, a wonderful experience. As a matter of fact, that year she was teacher of the year.

They had this banquet. They called in a lot of celebrities. Lewis was called in to address them, and they were singing all of these praises to this teacher, and she just sat there, terribly embarrassed. When she finally got up to speak she said, "You know, this makes me feel very bad, because I didn't do anything at all. Anybody could have done this. Why," she said, "when I looked at that roster, and I went right down the list, Alex Anderson 137, Bill Brooks 136, Charlie Carter 135. When I saw the IQs of these kids, I knew beyond any doubt I was going to have a wonderful year."

They told her that those were their locker numbers.

Do you think those kids loved that teacher? She treated them with courtesy and respect and had high expectations. That's why they loved her.

Who you are determines how you deal with people. She was confident in her ability as a teacher. She knew she had some raw material that would be marvelous students, so she was able to do a big job.

Relationships are important. Who you know makes a difference in your life, and who you know is the difference in your eternity.

When we look at relationships, when we understand the influence people have on us, we recognize that a lot of people influence us. Certainly your families had an impact on your life. Your teachers had an impact. Your employer and employees, your friends have an influence. As a matter of fact, the people that you are with influence you. We know, for example, that if you're child's friends are into drugs, the odds are nine times as great that your child will get involved in drugs.

You're impacted by the people around you. You can take a Southern boy or girl and send them up north. It's just a question of time before they'll pick up an accent. Or you can take a Northern boy or girl and send them down South, and pretty soon we'll have them talking normally. You're influenced by the people you are around.

Your faith has an impact on you. Your associates have an impact on you. Television, radio, and newspapers have an impact on you, and the books, tapes, magazines, and seminars that you read and listen to have an impact on you. Ultimately, those closest to me will determine my level of success.

The Los Angeles Times did a study several years ago, and they learned that the people who had made it big in this particular study, the people who had done the most with their life, at one point in their life made a definite decision to associate with the people that would further their careers—in other words, people of high moral character, people who had ambition, people who were sound in their character, people who were going places. They deliberately chose to associate with these people.

Sometimes on the job that's not possible, but in your free time, your time away from the job, you can definitely choose your associates, and that is so important.

Let's look at some of the things that we can do that will make a difference in our own lives. How can we increase our own motivation?

This week I was reading about a book, *Emotional Intelligence*, by Daniel Goleman. There are certain success factors that can't always be measured. We can measure your IQ, but he has something here called *emotional intelligence*. He writes: "It's crucial to your contentment, your career success, your marriage, your family life, and your children. An abundance of qualities of emotional intelligence lead to greater drive, self-discipline, caring, and cooperation."

What is emotional intelligence? He identifies it. "The hallmarks of emotional intelligence are the ability to know what you and those around you are feeling and to handle those feelings accordingly. Sensitivity is what we're talking about. This is a different way of being smart."

He goes ahead to say, "An abundance of the qualities that make for emotional intelligence leads to greater drive and self-discipline, caring, and cooperation, all of which makes our lives better and our streets safer. Those high in emotional abilities tend to be poised, outgoing, and cheerful. They have a strong commitment to people or causes, to taking responsibility, and to an ethical outlook. They are sympathetic with others. Their emotional lives are rich. In short, they're comfortable with themselves and the people around them. How well they handle emotional life determines their life destiny every bit as much as does their IQ."

Let me pause. They say self-praisers have scandal, but as old Izzy Dean used to say, "If you done it, it ain't bragging." You will have already noticed that the qualities he's talking about are those we have already identified and spelled out. Now what about that? How did it happen? When you have three sources, psychological, physiological, and theological, things like that just happen.

"If you want a happy, enduring marriage," Goleman says, "your EQ, not your IQ, can make the difference. Decades of marital research shows that it's how a couple handles emotional flashpoints, the hurts and irritations inevitable in any intimate relationship, that determines whether the marriage will last. The brightest among us can be emotional morons."

That's pretty direct, isn't it? The most stable unions are among couples who have found ways to address differences without escalating into personal attacks or retreating into stony silence. You'll never be rude with anyone you respect. That's in my book on courtship after marriage. I emphasize that you should make a friend out of your mate. You might say something mean, nasty, and ugly to your husband or wife, but you're not going to say anything mean, nasty, or ugly to your best friend. You just don't do that.

"They have mastered elements of emotional intelligence like empathy, listening without defensiveness, and criticizing without contempt or character assassination," Goleman writes. It really boils down, ladies and gentlemen, to claiming and using the qualities we have already identified.

What's the base upon which so much of life is built? It's hope. Hope is to the spirit what oxygen is to the brain. Again, John Maxwell says, "If there's hope in the future, there is power in the present."

What is hope? It's an honest optimism based on personal effort and encouragement. Adler says that hope is the foundational quality of any change, and what's the foundational quality of hope? What does hope need? It needs nourishment, it needs feeding, and it needs it on a regular basis. Encouragement keeps that hope alive. Encouragement then becomes the basic component of change in our lives.

To tie this together, I received something in the mail the other day, and it fascinates me a great deal. I don't even know who sent it to me, but it was a paper that was produced for counselors written by C.R. Snyder, and it's conceptualizing measuring and nurturing hope.

They added some psychological mumbo-jumbo. I call anything I don't clearly understand mumbo-jumbo, and that's what a lot of it was. Then it gets down to the nitty-gritty, and here's what he said. "Hope is the process of thinking about our goals and the way to achieve those goals.

"Higher-hope individuals report more mental energy and pathways for their goals, especially when there are blocks to those goals." To paraphrase somebody, he said, "When the going gets tough, the hopeful keep going." I hope people will undertake their goals with a focus on succeeding and will see roadblocks to these goals as being a normal part of life. They're going to happen.

We've already talked about that three or four times. "High-hope people have better outcomes in their lives. They have more difficult goals, greater success in achieving their goals. They see their goals as challenges, have greater happiness and less distress, have superior coping skills, recover better from physical injury, and report less burnout at work."

That's the reason I say you ought to read and reread this material. Anytime you need that word of encouragement, come back to this book and read a page or two. Don't wait until you get frustrated or discouraged. In heaven's name, don't wait till you get down. As I think you can understand, it's harder to get up than it is to stay up.

C.R. Snyder says, "Hope is not synonymous with intelligence, nor is it the same as being optimistic. It is more. High hope often assures the person of success in reaching goals. High intelligence may only give a person a chance." What about that?

You know that he said at the end? "Hope is ultimately counterproductive to the extent to which individuals pursue their goals to maximize their outcome to the comparative detriment of other people."

Do you hear that? It's negative if it's achieved at the detriment of somebody else. You cannot climb the ladder of success on the backs of others. It just can't happen.

We've talked about living well and finishing well. We've talked about the fact that we can move from stability to success and from success to significance. We've talked about what to do to survive in order to even get to the stability part.

The neat thing about all of this is that it enables you to take more control of your life. The basic problem is, we have so many people who are confused between personal growth and self-fulfillment. Self-fulfillment is the Dead Sea. It takes in lots of water and gives out nothing. It is dead. The river Jordan, for every drop of water it takes in, it gives out. The river Jordan is alive and well.

People who are givers are alive and well. Teachers who learn things so they can teach are much happier individuals. I'm not only talking about classroom teachers; all of us are teachers. The person who learns so they can teach others is a much happier individual than the one who learns so they can show up on a television quiz show and answer trivia questions. The personal-growth individual is learning so that everybody is going to benefit as a result.

Now think with me, if you will. Suppose everybody in your family and your company were to adopt the attitudes we've been talking about. I wonder what would happen. I know this involves a change, and change, you know, sometimes is painful, but then, as I've said earlier, so is unemployment and so is bankruptcy.

A lot of times I've had to explain people how to change when it's to their advantage. They change when they believe they can. They change when they have a plan of action, and they change when they can really see the possibilities and benefits for the future. But it takes training.

Sometimes somebody says, "Well, why should I train my employees and then lose them?" As I've said, one thing worse than training employees and losing them is not training them and keeping them. That gets to be very expensive.

Let me make it personal. We have sixty people on our staff; twenty of them are salespeople. They bring in money—very important people. The other forty don't sell anything, but every one of those forty is completely capable of killing a sale. Our switchboard operators can do it, our shipping department can do it, our accounting department can do it, our collection department can do it.

Which one of the groups should I train? We can measure what it costs to train somebody. There's no way we can measure what it costs *not* to train, because we don't know how much business they might run up.

The leadership objective, and we're talking relationships now, is to have every person on the payroll thinking about *my* company and *our* company, not *that* company or *the* company, because, ladies and gentlemen, everybody is important.

What would happen if every child in America were raised on the concepts we're talking about? What would happen if we adopt what I've called the immigrant's attitude?

I caught a cab in New Orleans several years ago. I'd been at a convention down there and was headed back to the airport. It was obvious to me that the driver was not from Mobile, Alabama. So I said to him, "Sir, where are you from?"

He said, "I'm from Nigeria."

"How long have you been in America?"

"Twelve years."

"Have you had a chance to get an education since you've been here?"

"Oh yes, as a matter of fact, I get my PhD in November. My wife has already gotten her master's."

"Well, my goodness alive, how did you happen to come to America?"

"When I was five years old, first day of kindergarten, they gave me an assignment. I had to go home, needed help, and I learned that day that my parents were both illiterate. As a five-year-old, I determined I was going to get an education."

"Five years old," I said, "that's awfully young to make that kind of decision."

"Yes, but I was so hurt by my parents' embarrassment that they couldn't help me that I determined that would never happen to me. A few years later, I decided to come to America."

"Have you supported your family?"

"Well, as you can see, I'm driving a taxi, but I've been a night watchman, I've loaded trucks, I've unloaded trucks, I've been a tutor. I have dug graves. I've done everything humanly possible, including being a tutor, in order to put bread on the table, and my wife has worked just as hard as I have."

"Do you have any children?"

"Yes, they're four, six, eight, and ten."

"I bet they're good students too," I said.

"The three that are in school are all honor students."

"What are you going to do now?"

"When I get my PhD, it's in business and finance and economics. I have a deal with a New York firm, a Wall Street firm. I'm going to work for them for two years, and then I'm going back where I have a very good job with the government, and that's where I will be."

I can only imagine how many nights there were when he desperately had to fight sleep in order to stay awake to get his assignments, or when a child would get sick and demanded a lot of extra attention. The demands on this man's and this woman's life were absolutely critical, but when they came to America, it was a dream fulfilled. They worked, and they worked awfully hard. Now, for the rest of their lives, they're going to have the benefits of that hard work.

All these things we've been talking about, do they work? I want to share with you a couple of additional things, because it is going to be extremely important to maintain the motivational momentum. As I said earlier, we need to run our day by the clock, our life with a vision. We need to be grateful for what happens in our life. Physician Hans Selye says, "The healthiest of all human emotions is gratitude."

In Houston, Texas, I was headed for breakfast early one morning. I caught a cab. It was only about three-quarters of a mile, but they advised me not to walk that time, since it was dark in that particular area of town. I got in the van, and as always, I greet people with enthusiasm. I said, "How are you doing?"

His verbatim answer was, "Praise God, I am in America."

I heard the doggonest sales talk on America in the next ten minutes I have ever heard in my life. This man had been a registered pharmacist, again from Nigeria. He was more excited, by far, about being a cab driver in America and more grateful for the opportunity.

He said, "I will get my license to be a pharmacist here, but in the meantime, I am having an absolutely wonderful time. I'm just so glad to be here."

The more you express gratitude for what you have, the more you will have to express gratitude for. It works the other way too. The more you gripe about the problems you have, my friend—I'll absolutely guarantee it—the more problems you will have to gripe about.

We need to express gratitude for our friends, our family, our job, our health, America. Again, the more you express gratitude for what you have, the more you will have to express gratitude for.

What you say to yourself is so incredibly important. The most important opinion you have is the opinion you have of yourself. The most important conversation you will ever have is the conversation that you will have with yourself.

When we look at the things we're talking about, I like to emphasize that you need to be realistic and practical in the things that you do. I believe that when I make statements, I am being absolutely pragmatic.

I love the story of the fellow in Tel Aviv. He was doing a tour of the Mann Center for the Performing Arts. The tour guide was really putting it on thick. It was a beautiful facility, granite and marble and tapestries and gold inlays and incredible paintings and acoustics.

Finally one of the tourists said, "I suppose this was named after Horace Mann, the famous author."

The tour guide said, "No, it was named after Frederick Mann from Philadelphia."

"Frederick Mann? Don't believe I've ever head of him. What did he write?"

The tour guide said, "A check."

Now that's being practical. That's being pragmatic.

I'm pragmatic. I was in Atlanta. A young man picked me up to take me down to the hotel where I was to be speaking, and he was going on and on about how it must be wonderful to have a company where your number-one objective in life is to help people be all they can be.

I said, "Young man, I appreciate the accolades, but you have it wrong. It's not my number-one objective."

"It's not your number-one objective?" he said. "What *is* your number-one objective?"

"It's to make a profit." I said. Samuel Gompers, an early labor leader, says that the number-one responsibility of a business is to make a profit. That's the only way you can stay in business. That's the only way those other sixty employees are going to have a job. It's the only way we can make a contribution to society, so our number-one objective is to make a profit so we can hit our number-one priority, which is to help people be all they can be.

There is that thing called a bottom line, and we learned several years ago that you can do a great deal more with profit than you can loss. Have you noticed that in your own life?

With integrity, you have nothing to fear, because you have nothing to hide. That is the most nerve-racking thing of all. Your creativity is stifled. Your productivity is destroyed. People that run from the law for years and finally get caught say, almost across the board, "What a relief."

I want to close with a little story about the most moving event that's happened in my life since I have been getting into the self-talk bit. You remember that we did talk about the biblical promises that are tied directly to this. The Bible really says you can be happier, you can be healthier, you can be more prosperous. You can be more secure, you can have more friends, you can have greater peace of mind, you can have those better family relationships, and yes, you can have hope.

I got into this self-talk at a convention down in New Orleans, Louisiana, back in January 1990. About six weeks later, I got one of the most moving letters I've ever received from anybody.

A mother was writing me and she said, "My daughter and I were in New Orleans. She took down and listed all the qualities of success, and every morning and every night, she stood in front of the mirror, and she claimed those. As a direct result of claiming these qualities, it led her back into the Bible. She made her peace with God, and on January 20, 1990, she was killed in an automobile accident, but she is safe today." She was only twenty-one years old.

My friends, I have to tell you, when something like that happens, you get the chill bumps all over you, but those gratitude bumps really come out big.

With these attitudes we've been talking about, taking this approach, putting other people first, there are going to be certain people that are going to laugh at you and say, "Man, you're different."

Let me remind you the little world laughed, but the big world gathered on the banks of the Hudson when Robert Fulton went steaming by. The little world laughed, but the big world was tuned in when Alexander Graham Bell completed that phone call. The little world laughed, but the big world was at Kitty Hawk when the Wright brothers took that first flight into the air, which forever changed the world we're in.

Some people might laugh at some of the things we're suggesting that you do here, but I'm here to tell you the big world is going to be standing on the sidelines, cheering you with incredible enthusiasm. And the big thing is, it's not what you get by reaching your destination. It's what you *become* by reaching that destination that is the important thing.

Buy these ideas. Take these steps. Follow these procedures, because if you do, I will see you not just at the top. Hey, I'm going to see you over the top. God bless you.

CHAPTER **6**

Building and Maintaining a Winning Attitude

It's a fact of life that everybody has the right attitude occasionally. The question is, how do you maintain that attitude in a world where you have a lot of negatives?

I heard about a college professor who was told by his wife one morning as he headed off for college to teach his classes, "You know, today we're moving. Here's the address of the new house. We're not going to be here when you get here. Go to the new house."

"No problem," he said.

That afternoon, he showed up at the old house, and it was empty. Didn't see anybody there. Then he looked in the neighbor's yard, and they had a little boy playing. He called him. He said, "Son, do you know the family that did live here?"

"Oh, yes, sir. I know them quite well."

"Do you have any idea where they've gone?"

The little boy said, "Yes, sir. I do. As a matter of fact, mom told me you would probably forget."

I talk about a positive attitude. This really is the right life attitude. Some things don't necessarily call for positive thinking, but all things call for right thinking, mature thinking, sound thinking. This is the way we go through life. We need the right thing as far as our job is concerned, we need the right attitude with our family, our company, our community, our country.

I love what Chuck Swindoll said:

The longer I live, the more I realize the impact of attitude on life. Attitude, to me, is more important than facts. It is more important than the past, than education. It is more important than money, than circumstances, than failures, than successes, than what other people think or say or do. It is more important than appearance, gifted ability, or skill. It will make or break a company, a church, or a home. The remarkable thing is we have a choice every day regarding the attitude we will embrace from that day. We cannot change our past. We cannot change the fact that people will act in a certain way. We cannot change the inevitable. The only thing that we can do is play on the one string that we have, and this string is attitude. I am convinced that life is 10 percent what happens to me and 90 percent how I react to it, and so it is with you. We are in charge of our attitudes.

Attitudes are important. Today we hear a lot of talk about pushing the envelope, playing it close to the edge, and all of those other things. The American worker is recognized as being the most productive worker in the world, but if you were to look at corporate America at 8:00 in the morning, if they're supposed to be at work at 8:00, at one minute to 8:00, you see a real helter-skelter affair going on in most offices and plants. They're in a dead run to get there. They're walking huffing and puffing. They hustle back and get a cup of coffee, and they scoot back to their work station, and by the time they start to work, it's ten minutes after starting time.

If you were to look in on corporate America with a videotape at 5:00 in the afternoon, you would see the American worker all lined up in a three-point stance, and at 5:00, man alive, do they ever get out.

That's OK if that's what they really want to do, but it's the little things that make the big difference. My watch is four hours wrong. I don't have a problem with it. I can tell you at 3:00 in the morning if it's four hours wrong, but if it's four minutes wrong, then I have a problem. If my plane is supposed to leave at 11:06, and I get there at 11:10, well, you get the picture. I made a deal with the airlines years ago that if I wasn't there when they got ready to go, they were just to go ahead without me. I found out that they live up to their end of the agreement.

I'm not necessarily advocating this business of getting there early, but I am saying that you might just get there ten minutes early, casually take the necessary equipment that you need to get started, and get the cup of coffee, and the moment your paycheck starts, your workday starts. You work until 5:00. Then you pack up to leave.

That's not a heavy burden, but if you do that, instead of being caught in the mass of people running out at 5:00, when your life is in danger—they talk about danger on the freeway, but the danger is getting out of the building and out of the parking lot. Ten minutes later, you can leave in peace and quiet and safety, and I'll tell you something else. The boss is looking. They really are.

Do we give a little extra? It's the part of the blanket that hangs over the bed that keeps you warm. If you don't believe that, you've never been in the service and been short-sheeted. You call a girl a kitten, you score all kind of points. Call her a cat, and I don't need to tell you, you have a problem. It's the little things that make a difference. Call her a vision, and you're home free; call her a sight and oh, brother.

I was so amused when the last presidential election took place, and three outstanding candidates were talking about family values, and interestingly enough, they never were able to identify the family values they discussed back and forth.

I challenge you to look at the qualities we've already identified and ask yourself if you wouldn't love to have a husband or a wife with all those qualities.

Wouldn't you love to have kids with all those qualities? Wouldn't you love to have every teacher in our education system and every administrator with all those qualities? Wouldn't you love to have a boss and employees with all of those qualities? Wouldn't you love to have every politician in American from dog catcher right on up with those qualities?

The reality, you see, is that none of those are just family values or just business values or just educational values. They're all life values. Check the records. The qualities that make a person a good husband or a good wife will also make them a better employee or a better office holder or a better FBI agent or a better whatever they do in life. I challenge you to locate one quality there that you would not want your child taught in school—with the possible exception of faith. But would you want your child to be taught everything else? What kind of child would you be raising? I can guarantee you it would be a magnificent child.

As you've probably noticed, I'm talking about a lot of things that take time. It takes time to claim these qualities. It takes time to be nice and courteous to people. It takes time to do your job. It takes a little time to get there a few minutes earlier and stay a little bit longer, but the reality is that we do not have a shortage of time. Everybody in America has exactly the same amount: twenty-four hours a day. What we do have is a lot of problems with our direction.

Again, I refer you to the day-before-vacation attitude, when you got so much more done simply because you had organized that time in an entirely different way.

Now the question is, are we really affected by what goes into our mind? *Reader's Digest* recently had an interesting article that pointed out that 31 percent of the kids in America between ages four and six, if given a choice, would prefer the television set over their dad. Ladies and gentlemen, that is frightening, to say the least.

Let me ask you a question. Have you ever gone to a movie and laughed? Have you ever gone to a movie and cried? Do you think it's because they put something in the seats, or was it because they put something on the screen that went in your mind, that affected your thinking, that aroused you emotionally? That's what I'm talking about here.

People pay more attention to what you do than what you say. They won't believe everything you say always, but they will believe everything that you do. You can absolutely count on it. You know life sometimes brings some interesting challenges, interesting opportunities, I guess I should say.

I heard about this fellow that was playing golf. He was on the first tee, and he stepped up, teed that ball up, and busted that sucker about 200 yards straight and about 150 yards to the right. One of the pros was riding with him, and he said, "We're not going to be able to find that one. Let's just go ahead."

So the fellow teed up again. He hit another one, and as they were putting out on the first green, they saw this cart coming down at breakneck speed. It was another one of the assistant pros, and he was really riding down there. He came up to the green and said, "Who hit that horrendous slice that went all the way over? The governor's wife was playing golf with me, and she was in the cart. We were in the wood, and it hit her right upside the head. Who hit that horrendous slice?"

This guy very timidly said, "I did."

The other assistant pro said, "I want you to know that I talked to the governor, and he is enormously upset. He is furious."

The guy said, "What do you think I should do?"

"You should play it a little more off your left toe, and strengthen your grip. That's what you ought to do."

Sometimes things come out a little different than we thought.

OK—now to maintain the right mental attitude, that's the key. You do it by reversing the way you get out of bed. I'm not talking about getting out of bed backwards, but you know the way most people get out of bed, the alarm clock—it's misnamed, it really is an opportunity clock. If you can hear that, it gives you an opportunity to get up and go, and if you can't hear it, that might mean you done got up and gone. Depending on what you believe, that can be very bad.

Anyway, that alarm clock sounds off. People generally reach over, they finally find it, they turn it off, and then they slap their face and say, "Honey, is it already time to get up? It seems like we just lay down. I'm going to go to bed earlier tonight. I can't take it." No, I haven't been at your home visiting. That's just the way a whole lot of people do it.

Instead of doing that, let's reverse the way you get out of bed. The opportunity clock sounds off for you. You reach over and shut it off. I think that is very important. You sit straight up on the side of your bed, and you slap your hands, and you say, "Oh, boy. It's a great day to get up and go to work today."

There you are, two-thirds asleep. Your hair is all down in your eyes. You're trying to slap your hands, and sometimes you hit it, and sometimes you miss it, and you say, "Oh, boy, it's a good day to get up and go to work."

Hey, friend, that ain't the way you feel at all, but let me tell you something: You do not decide to get up when the clock goes off. You decided that when you set the clock. What you decide now is *how* you're going to get up. Are you going to get up with excitement and enthusiasm, or are you going to get up looking like the picture on your driver's license? You have to decide.

Now, despite the fact that you might not really feel that good, you are up. That's where you made the decision to be the night before. Then you go in the shower, and while you're taking that shower, you do a little singing, and I know what a lot of people's voices are, but it's amazing what will happen.

What you're doing when you sow an action is something that is psychologically very sound. You don't think about it. You just do it. It's an instinct, it's a reflex when you do this a while. You hop on the side of the bed. You sow an action, you reap a habit. You sow a habit, you reap a character. You sow a character, you reap a destiny.

A number of years ago, I had a lady eighty-five years old say to me, "When you told me that, I thought that was the silliest thing I had ever heard a grown man say. I'm eighty-five years old, and you want me to get up on the side of the bed and slap my hands like a child. Why, that's silly, and I knew it was. But, you know, I lay down that night, and I thought, I do live by myself, and nobody's going to know about it but me. Why not?"

You're only young once in your life, and she was one of these people that qualifies as being a youngster. So the next morning that alarm clock sounded. She said, "I sat up on the side of the bed, and I drew back to slap my hand, but I couldn't do it. I got so tickled, and I laughed at myself all day long." She'd had a wonderful day.

Have you ever participated in organized team sports? Have you ever gone out for practice when you just flat did not want to go out for practice? You ever get out there and say, "Well, the coach said he's going can me if I ever miss another practice. I'm out here, but I'm not going to do anything. He ain't watching me anyhow.'" After you've been out there about ten minutes, you say, "Well, as long as I'm here—"

Have you ever gone out for a practice feeling awful, and ten minutes later felt good? A lot of people say, "When I get motivated, I'll do it." Hey, friend, you got it backwards. Do it, and you'll feel like doing it. You'll be motivated then to do it.

You take that action. Start the day like that. Do I do this every day? Nope. Did I used to do it? Yes. Do I want to do it now? Don't need to, but let me tell you something. If I get a late wake-up call somewhere and I have to get out of bed and run, I hop up, I slap my hands and say, "Yippee!" I head for the shower. It really does get you moving a whole lot faster.

Now, if you have gotten up early enough, you need to make a phone call. Call somebody whom you love, admire, and respect. Call that person and simply say, "You know, I've been thinking about you, and I just wanted you to know how much I appreciate you as an individual. You're one of the people that has had a big influence on my life. You really are an asset to your community. You're a credit to the profession you're in. Just wanted to call you and say thank you for being my friend."

Something happens. First of all, your friend is tremendously encouraged, but second, you're inspired. Psychologically and theologically, you're on sound ground; physiologically, you're on sound ground. When you do this early in the morning, it jump-starts the flow of serotonin in your brain, and that's the feel-good neurotransmitter. You feel good about yourself when you do something nice for somebody else.

I have a speaker friend. He heard me go through this one time, and he thought, "I'm going to give it a shot. I ain't going to do it in the morning, but I will do it at night." Every Saturday night, he calls somebody whom he hasn't talked to in some little while, and he'll just tell them how much he appreciates them. He said, "Zig, it's been one of the most gratifying things in my life." He said, "The first time I did it, it took me forty-five minutes to get that dude off the telephone. He was so excited and so encouraged."

What are we doing? Again, we're putting that other person in an important position. They feel good about it, and you feel good about it too. Make that telephone call. It will make a difference in their lives.

I've talked a lot about values. I've talked about how you can have everything in life you want if you just help enough other people get what they want. In a recent issue of *Fortune* magazine, they listed the ten wealthiest people in the world. One of the men they listed was a Chinese gentleman from Hong Kong who is worth $5.9 billion. He's the ninth-wealthiest man in the world. Incidentally, he got his start selling plastic toys on the street. He has an interesting philosophy. He has two sons, and he's taught them the same philosophy.

He is a deal maker. He does joint ventures with people, and he's taught them and has always believed that if 10 percent of the deal for financing it is a fair share but you could get 12 percent, take 9 percent. He said that is good because, number one, it gives them a better chance of making it, so it makes your investment safer. Number two, word will get around, and instead of getting one 12 percent deal, you'll get a dozen 9 percent deals.

The next thing to do if you really want to maintain the right attitude is learn how to greet people. I was rather amused this evening as I was coming in a few minutes before 7:00. I greeted a number of you, always the same way, "Good morning." Most of you responded, "Good morning." Whether I'm in Auckland, New Zealand or Augusta, Maine, whether it's 9:00 in the morning or 9:00 in the evening, on average 85 percent of them will respond, "Good morning." Then almost immediately they'll say, "It's not morning."

I'll say, "Then why did you say *morning*?"

"Because you said *morning*."

I say, "That makes a really neat point." You see, you go out in life to find friends, they're very scarce. You go out in life to be a friend, you find them everywhere. What you send out is exactly what you're going to get back.

I believe the Good Book says, "As you sow, so also shall you reap." The computer people are terribly negative. They say, "Garbage in, garbage out." Us folks who are optimistic, upbeat, and positive say, "You put the good stuff in, you get the good stuff out. Send the good stuff out to get the good stuff back." It's the law. That is simply the way it works.

When you greet people, greet them with excitement and enthusiasm. If they beat you to it and say, "Good morning. How are you doing?" then you need to be absolutely honest. You say, "Better than good. How are you doing?" or "Super good, but I'll get better," instead of the way that most people do it:

"How are you doing?"

"Fine, since it's Friday."

Or "Good, since it's payday," or "Great, since the weather is fine today." Don't you just love it when they pull themselves up and say, "Well, under the circumstances . . ."? It makes you wonder what they're doing under there in the first place, don't it?

When somebody asks you how you are doing, be honest. Say, "Outstanding, but I'm improving." You might say, "Well, Zig, suppose I'm not doing outstanding. Am I telling the truth?" Yes, you're telling the truth. You're just telling it in advance, that's all.

"But is that honest?" you might ask. Well, I bring the theology into it. God's Son himself did that. He said, "I thank you, Father, for what you're going to do." You're just telling the truth in advance. That's all that you're doing, and so you give them that very positive answer.

Occasionally I'll have somebody say, "Zig, do people always react favorably to that?" No, we have some folks that are a little bit—anyhow, everybody knows everybody doesn't respond that way.

Several years ago, a good buddy of mine and I were going down to a cafeteria, and it was about 1:30. In cafeterias, by about 1:30 the lunch crowd is over, and you just have stragglers going through. This was one of those brutally hot days (not at all typical of Dallas; it just happened to be happening in Dallas). A gentleman in front of us was doing what I always do.

A number of years ago, my youngest daughter, Julie, as a teenager got a job in a cafeteria. Up until then, I had taken those folks working there for granted. I didn't realize just what a tough job they had, but when my daughter went to work there, I noticed something very interesting.

I noticed that if the people behind the counter were pleasant and courteous but delayed the line at all, management said, "Move them along. Move them along." If they gave them too much, management fussed. If they didn't give them enough food, the customer fussed. It's a tough job. So I made a decision that never again would I ever go down a cafeteria line without saying something pleasant and courteous to whoever was behind the line.

Now an interesting thing happens. By the time I've gone down the line four or five times, you can watch the ladies down on the other end, and almost invariably they're nudging each other and saying, "There he is." If you were to go with me to lunch in that cafeteria where we've been four or five times, I guarantee you that on the dishes where they have an option, where they scoop it up, I'll get 25 percent more to eat than you will.

You can have what you want if you help enough other people get what they want, but that's not the motive behind it. I should be getting less, not more, but that's their way of saying, "Thank you for treating me like a human being."

Anyway, on this particular brutally hot day, we were walking down the line. The gentleman in front of me had gone to the same school I had, and he was greeting people positively and optimistically. He got to the lady cutting the roast beef, and he asked her, "How are you doing?" You do know that some people perspire and some people sweat. Well, this gal that was cutting the roast beef, she was sweating.

When he said, "How are you doing?" she wiped her hand across her forehead, and it was loaded with sweat. She slung it on the floor, and she said, "It has been one of those days."

She wasn't talking to me, but she was talking about my day, the only one I have, and if you don't think every day is important, you just try missing one of them. She was talking here in my city. I had a reputation at stake. I couldn't let her abuse the day like that, so I said, "Yes, it's absolutely magnificent, isn't it?" She looked at me with disgust mingled with contempt as she said, "You have been out in the sun too long."

"No, to tell you the truth," I said, "I just got back from overseas. I've seen poverty like you cannot possibly imagine. I've seen men and women with nothing to eat and children with no clothes to wear. I've seen sanitation conditions that would absolutely turn your stomach, and I look at you, and you're young, and you're healthy, and you're pretty, and you're working, and you live in America. I know it in my own mind because I've seen so many cases of it happening: you can take this job you have right here, doing exactly what you're doing, and doing it to the absolute best of your ability, and they will move you up because the one controlling factor in the growth of any organization is quality, skilled, gung-ho, motivated people.

"You could someday be the manager of this cafeteria. Who knows? Someday some investors might be attracted to your personality and the way you do things, and you might be given an opportunity to become a part owner in a business, because this is America."

Personally, I thought it was pretty good. That's right off the top of my head. Hey, what do you expect? I knew that she wanted to express her undying gratitude for the fact that I'd so unwillingly and unselfishly given my time and my effort to make her lot in life better. So I looked at her and said, "Now you feel better, don't you?"

She said, "You are sick."

Well, you win some, you lose some, and some are rained out. So I tucked my tail between my legs, and me and my buddy went on down. We sat down, and, like I say, it was brutally hot. I quickly finished off the glass of tea, and there was a little lady about sixty-five or seventy years old; she was one big wrinkle. I'd never seen anything quite like it. I've also never seen eyes that were more beautiful and alive and dancing than what I was witnessing with her. She came up to me and said, "Can I get you some more tea?"

"You bet," I said. "How are you doing?"

She did a little two-step backwards and said, "Honey, if it was any better, I'd think the deck was stacked."

"Well," I said, "why don't you go tell the ladies on the serving line?"

Then she expressed a wisdom that really was astonishing. She said, "No, pardon. If I fool around with those girls very long, I might be just like they are."

Very true. Solomon said, "If you want to be wise, you run with the wise. If you want to be a fool, you run with fools."

We are affected by the people that we are around. There is no question about that. You want to build that winning attitude? You want to maintain it and keep things going in a positive way? Then you need to understand everybody you deal with is a person.

I heard about a fellow that returned a phone call. The person at the other end picked it up and said, "286-7145." The gentleman said, "Yes, I'd like to speak with John Anderson." The person at the other end said, "Well, who is this?" He said, "It's 233-9191."

People say, "Ziglar, where do you get all your stories?" Most of them happened to me.

About six months ago, I was running pretty close to departure time. I checked in at the counter, and as soon as the person saw my name, got on the little PA system to the people in the plane and said, "3C is here." I was seated in seat 3C.

"Well," I thought, "now I really am a number, but at least I got a letter to go along with the number. I'm 3C." I went in and sat down and got airborne. They came around to take the orders for lunch. The attendant came to me, and I said, "I believe you have a special meal for me." He turned to the other person and said, "Fat-free is here." So I'm 3C and fat-free in case anybody asks.

The way you greet people in person is important. The way you greet people on the telephone is extremely important also. I challenge you: two of you get together, look up ten numbers of businesses in wherever you live, and swap numbers. Don't put the name of the businesses down. When you dial those ten numbers, you will be unable to identify more than three of them based on the way they answer the telephone: "[Blank] Company," and you don't have any more idea than a goat as to what the number is or who the company is.

At our company when the phone rings, our ladies pick it up, and say with a lot of enthusiasm, "Good morning." Then they make a motivational speech—

not nearly as long as the ones I make, but they make a motivational speech. "It's a great day."

People always ask me, "Is it always a great day?" You bet it is. Years ago, we decided it's going to be a great day today. Then "it's a great day at Zig Ziglar's. This is Barbara," or "This is Lu. How may I direct your call?" The entire length of the conversation is six seconds.

It's astonishing how much time that will save. It is astonishing how much better a response you get, because as you know, some people in some parts of the country just flat talk funny. When the first few words on a telephone call are made, most people do not understand them. It has nothing to do whether they're hard of hearing or not. But when we say, "Good morning," because that's so generally familiar, they respond to that.

Then, when we say, "It's a great day," now we have their entire attention, and when we identify the company, then it does make a difference. They do get the word.

When I'm at home—and I stress that this is when I'm at home—I answer the phone in a different way. I might pick it up and answer it singing or with "It's a beautiful day," or "Good morning to you."

A lot of time they'll say, "Who is this?"

I'll say, "It's whoever you want. Who do you want?"

"My, you sure do feel good."

I'll say, "Yes." Like I said earlier, I decided a long time ago I was going to feel good today. I might pick it up and say, "Hidy, hidy, hidy."

My favorite way of answering the telephone is "Good morning, this is Jean Ziglar's happy husband." I do it for two reasons. Number one, it is the truth. Number two, fellows, you cannot believe how many points I score with that redhead when I answer the telephone that way, and I like to score points with the redhead.

When my grandchildren were small and coming along, I would use it this way. My first three granddaughters were Sunshine—I nickname them all. Second was Keeper—you know, when a fisherman pulls in a good one, he knows he has a keeper. The third one was Little Lover, and the fourth one is Promise. Now Keeper is babysitting Promise, so she's a promise keeper. She was the one who pointed that out to me.

Whenever the grandchildren were around, I'd pick up the telephone. I'd say, "Good morning, this is Keeper's proud granddaddy," or "Good morning, this is Sunshine's proud granddaddy." You ought to see their little eyes just dancing there. It is something.

When our son was a youngster, we'd pick up the telephone. The phone rang one day, and I said, "Good morning, this is Tom Ziglar's proud pop." A little voice from Sam Wing, who lived down the street, came on, and he said, "Is Tom there, he-he?"

I said, "Yes."

He said, "Can I speak to him, he-he?"

I said, "Yes. Tom."

Then Sam turned to his parents and said, "Boy, they have a weird way of answering the telephone."

But I noticed something rather interesting. From then on, every time I'd pull my car into the driveway, old Sam would see it, and two seconds later the telephone would ring. I'd answer it that way, and old Sam would say, "Is Tom there, he-he? Is Tom there?" He didn't want to talk to Tom. He wanted to hear me answer the telephone.

You might say, "What's the big deal?" Remember we talked about personal life, our family life, and our business life? Let me tell you what this does to the family. It creates an environment. See, kids are going to go where they're welcome. They're going to go where there's love. They're going to go where there's excitement.

We used to have our den filled with youngsters from all over, many of them coming in just to see who this strange couple were. But I'd rather be serving a dozen of the kids Coca-Cola in my den than having somebody else serving my children coke in their den. See, kids are going to join gangs.

The rest of the story with Sam Wing is, Sam was overweight, and we became friends. I was doing a lot of jogging. Sam started jogging with me. He lost all of the weight. When he was a junior at Notre Dame University, I got one of the most beautiful letters. He said, "You know, my family and I have always been close," and his family is loving and close, but he said, "I just want you to know that the impact your family, you and your wife, had on my life made a substantial difference."

We touch and affect people wherever we go, in whatever we do. Answering that telephone creates an environment for our children and for our family. It does make a difference.

You might say, "That's out of character for me." Well, let me just say we can make it *not* out of character for you. When you act out a little of that, the first thing you know you will be that way.

I'm really talking about consideration for others. You know, there's an African saying that it takes a whole village to raise a child. The Babema tribe in South Africa has the most unusual custom. When somebody does something of a criminal nature or an antisocial nature, they try that person in front of the entire village. Anybody there, from children on up, who is old enough to voice themselves will confront the person who's done the antisocial thing.

It might, first of all, be a little seven-year-old girl. She'll say, "You know, I was really surprised to learn what you had done, because I remember that you're the first one who taught me how to bait a hook, and I remember how I used to sit on your lap around a fire in the evening. I always felt so good when you were around."

Maybe a ten-year-old would come out and say, "You're the one who taught me how to read the trails.

I couldn't believe you did what you did." The only criticism was none. They always pointed out all of the good things that person had done. It is said that almost never is there a case where the offender ever does anything of an antisocial nature again.

Sydney Harris put it this way, "Have you ever noticed when people say I'm going to tell you something for your own good, they proceed to tell them something bad?" I wonder what the impact would be if we kept it good.

As I said earlier, how much better would this be instead of telling a child, "You keep that up, one of these days you're going to go to jail, boy"? Bill Glass says over 90 percent of the people incarcerated were repeatedly told by their parents that was what was going to happen.

To repeat myself—but I think this is so important—what would happen if we were to say to the child, "If you keep studying your lessons like that, one of these days you'll win a scholarship to a university"? "You keep treating people that way, you'll have friends everywhere you go. You keep working like that, and one day you'll be the president of your own company." You put in what you want to get out.

If you want to maintain that marvelous winning attitude, you need to adopt some symbols. They have them on every street corner, it seems, in America. I mentioned earlier that some people call them red lights, some call them stop lights, and some call them traffic lights. You're going to spend twenty-seven hours a year in front of the go lights waiting for the right color to come along.

Have you ever been sitting there waiting on the right color to come along? You're all excited, you're enthused, you're motivated, and you're going to spend twenty-seven hours a year there. You look out the side of your eye, and you see some dude over there. He's waiting on the color to change too, but he has a good, firm grip on that steering wheel. I mean, he doesn't want it to go anywhere. He fixes his mouth just in case he has to talk to that light.

Then—you can't believe this, but there's some people who will actually put their foot on the accelerator and race the engine trying to change the color of the light.

Now I hate to be negative. As a matter of fact, I'm not going to be negative. I'll be like the little boy who came home from school one day and said, "Dad, I'm afraid I flunked my arithmetic test." His dad said, "Son, that's negative. Be positive." He said, "Dad, I'm positive I flunked that arithmetic test."

I'm not going to be negative. I want to be positive when I say racing that engine ain't going to change the color of that light, folks. I have a good friend, Bernie Lofchick, and compared to him, I'm one of the negatives of life. Bernie is a positive guy. He's so positive, he's never had a cold. On occasion, he's had a warm. He won't even talk about the weekend. He calls it the strong-end.

You might say, "Come on, Ziglar. Go lights, warms, strong-ends. Is all of that necessary?"

You can be mediocre without it.

"Mediocre? What's old Zig talking about? I'm the president of my own company. Mediocre? I'm worth over $7 million. Mediocre? I have my PhD. Mediocre? I was number one in sales for the last three years running."

Bully for you, but I still say *mediocre*—maybe.

Success is not measured by what you do compared to what somebody else does. You might have ten times their ability. Success is measured by what you do compared to what you are capable of doing with what God has given you. That's what success really is. I'm not saying you have to be the best in the whole world, but I am saying you do your best.

I'm not talking about beating anybody. I'm talking about being number one with the most important person on earth, and that is you. When you can look in that mirror every night and say, "Boy, I gave it my best shot. I did my best," you're going to find that that is more than good enough for accomplishing some incredible objectives in life. I'm talking about using the ability you have.

What do you do when you encounter difficulty? There are a lot of difficulties. Some are what we call the fender-benders of life. What's a fender-bender? Maybe the electricity went off, as it did in west Texas this afternoon.

Incidentally just as a matter of interest, one young man that had interviews, he was heading for the airport. He said, "The traffic lights"—he didn't call them *go lights*—"were off, and it was chaos."

You see, when you identify them as go lights, you literally are telling the truth. You know what happens when the lights go off, and there's no patrolman there to direct the traffic. So if somebody ever asks you for directions, don't tell him to go down to the third stop light. Tell him to go down to the third go light and make the turn. You can't say it with a straight face, I guarantee you.

The instant you say "go light," your mind is back on this recording, and it really will trigger the second thought and the third thought and the fourth thought, because the mind is an associating machine when you have those little fender-benders.

My good friend Clebe McClary, who lives over in South Carolina, a genuine American hero. He takes what he calls the FIDO approach—F-I-D-O. If it's just a fender-bender in life, you forget it and drive on. There are some things that are not worth making a big deal about.

I heard about a fellow that went in a restaurant and ordered some soup. The waiter brought it out, and the guy looked at the waiter and said, "I can't eat this soup." He said, "I'll get the manager." The manager came over, and he said to the manager, "I can't eat this soup."

The manager said, "I'll get the chef." The chef came out, and the guy said, "I can't eat this soup." The chef said, "What's the problem?" He said, "I don't have a spoon." It wasn't a big deal, but until he identified what the problem was, he really couldn't eat that soup, could he?

Say you're a little down; maybe you have a case of the blahs. You know, blahs are seldom fatal, but you're just not feeling 187 percent. So if somebody asks how you're doing, you can say, "Not real good at the moment, but at 3:30 this afternoon, man, I'm going to be great."

They'll say, "Well, what's going to happen at 3:30?"

"I'm going to feel great."

"Now wait a minute, let me get this straight. You don't feel good now, but at 3:30 you're going to feel good?"

"Absolutely."

"If you are going to feel good at 3:30, why don't you go ahead and feel good now?"

"Absolutely not. I worked hard for this misery. Nobody's going to talk me out of it. I'm entitled to it. You might as well forget it. I'm going to feel bad until then, and then I'm going to feel good."

"That's silly. Why are you going to wait until 3:30?"

"All right, I'll tell you what I'll do. I'll move it up to 3:00, but not another minute sooner."

You might say, "That's silly." Of course it is, and that's why it's funny. You start laughing, my friends, there go the blahs. That'll get you out of those cases absolutely guaranteed.

The next thing you want to do is look at how you can utilize your time more effectively. We talk a lot about that in the goal series, and goals are important because it's been rightly said, "If you don't plan your future, it's a pretty good indication you're not interested in it." If we just wait for the future to happen, to let it unfold, it's not going to unfold in the best possible way.

How do you maintain that right attitude? One thing you do is take advantage of what I call *two-fers*. What's a two-fer? A two-fer is getting that college education while you're in Automobile University. That's in your car. As you're riding along—the average American will spend over ten hours a week in his automobile—you can learn an awful lot of things. In other words, you don't just sit there to get there.

On the way, you get a very powerful message, and I will give you a specific example in a few minutes that will make a difference. Listen in your car. You take something to read any time you go to get in any kind of line. When I head for the airport, I have a book, a small paperback or a pamphlet or something I'm very interested in, in case I have to get in a line. I'm not just going to stand there and stew or sit there and wait. I'm going to be doing something while I'm there.

As a matter of fact, when I get on the airplane to go somewhere, I'm a total workaholic, because when

I get home, I want to have time to do some of the things I enjoy doing, so I do a lot of two-fers.

I'm a football fan. Really I'm a Cowboys fan. When I'm watching the Cowboys, I'm always in two-fers. I either have my whole family around me, and we're having a wonderful time being together, or if I happen to be watching it by myself, the average play in professional football lasts less than six seconds. That's right. They have 120 plays in a game. That's between 600 and 700 seconds. That's between ten and twelve minutes. The game takes three hours.

During that other two hours and fifty minutes, I will average reading well over 100 pages, or I will put together an outline, and I don't miss any part of the game itself. If I happen to be glancing down when a play starts, I'll catch it on the replay, because I guarantee you if anything happens, they're going to have a replay. That's a two-fer that I use.

One thing you can do to save a whole lot of time is promise yourself that you will get rid of your channel changer. Seventy percent of the time when we watch television, we have no interest whatever in what we're seeing, and we're channel hopping. Two hours later, you can't even remember what you were watching in the first place.

Get the *TV Guide* out. You'd be amazed at how much time that'll save you. Make your choices, and then say, "I'm going to watch this." Turn to that channel, and when you get through watching it, turn it off. Does that require discipline? Yes. It's a choice that we make, and that choice is a very important one. Get rid of the channel changer. You definitely need to know what you're watching and why you're watching it.

You need to do a lot of reading. That's one thing you can do for growing. A lot of people say, "I do not have a college education." Here's some interesting information. If you're an average reader, and you read thirty minutes a day—now that's not all the time in the world—if you read thirty minutes a day, in your lifetime, ladies and gentlemen, you will have read over 1,000 books. That's the equivalent of going through college five times. You won't have the degree, but you'll have the knowledge.

I like to emphasize that what you do *off* the job determines how far you go *on* the job. How do you utilize that time otherwise? Think about the importance of structure, and you think about what my daughter was saying about using the Performance Planner to keep everything up to date.

There are 168 hours in a week. Two areas of your life—your health and earning a living—require roughly 120 of those 168 hours. There are seven nights in the week. If you sleep eight hours, there go fifty-six of them. If you eat even for only two hours, there go another fourteen of them. There go seventy hours right there taking care of your health. If you're doing any exercising at all, add a couple or three hours to that.

If you work forty hours a week, eight hours a day, your preparation and driving time to get to your job, your preparation to come back home, and reading and other things you do outside the job, your forty-hour week means at least fifty, maybe sixty hours a week.

Subtract that from the 168, and you're going to have family time, exercise time, recreation time. If you're going to have personal-growth time, hey, you have to get that time organized. That's why I keep saying keep listening, because motivation is the spark that lights the fire of knowledge. It fuels the engine of accomplishment, and it maximizes and maintains momentum. That's what motivation really does.

To motivate is to pull out or to draw out. As I said earlier, why did you get so much more done on the day before vacation than you do on a normal day? First of all, you had planned the day. Second, you were excited about doing it. Third, you accepted the responsibility for being there and performing. Fourth, you were disciplined in staying right with the task. Fifth, you decisively moved from one task to another.

Bottom line is, you got an awful lot more done. You were excited about doing it. Now, to maintain the excitement, Shad Helmstetter says, "You can't change from a negative mind-set to a positive mind-set without changing from negative talking to positive talking. To do that, you must change the input from negative to positive."

Your input does influence your outlook. Your outlook does influence your output. Your output does determine what your future is going to be.

I got a five-page letter from Stephen Payne from Bartlesville, Oklahoma. Finished high school, age twenty-three. He enrolled in Automobile University. He now speaks Spanish, French, and Italian fluently. He translates for his company in Spanish and French. He's taken up German and Japanese. He's now also going into Latin, and later he says he's going to learn his own Cherokee language.

Let me tell you a little bit more about him. According to what he said, he tried to commit suicide. He had a full tank of gas. He lay down outside the car in the garage underneath the exhaust pipe. A seventeen-year-old boy who was a friend of his couldn't get anybody to come to the door and called his mother. They came to him, and hey said he realized that when his life was saved, maybe it was for a purpose.

He does a lot of positive self-talk. One thing he's saying is "I forgive everyone, everything, and especially myself, so I live fully and joyfully in the present moment."

Second, he's utilizing Automobile University to the fullest. A lot of this got started when he started listening to our series on goals. The thing that made the difference, though, was when he watched our video entitled "Changing the Picture," and he got a clear idea of what he was going to look like.

He set another goal: to weigh 155 pounds. Before he ever takes a bite to eat, he always asks himself, "Would a skinny person eat this?" It's amazing what that will do.

Now let me tell you why he tried to commit suicide. He'd lost hope. That's when people want to end it all. There's no hope. Hope was born again with the fact that he was saved, and he said, "I do have a purpose." Then he recognized that he needed to feed that encouragement in there in order to maintain the hope.

What does this philosophy really do in life? I got a letter on January 30, 1995 from a gentleman down in Tampa, Florida. His name is Alan Sowell. It's a lengthy letter, but it talks about all the things that we believe are important: how can you really be happy, healthy, prosperous? Can you really get more of the things money will buy and all of the things that money won't buy? He wrote:

I saw you in Dallas on March 31, 1994. That was a success seminar. I listened to what you said about the real estate agent whose income went up 500 percent and who used to be late for everything, and hasn't been late since he started using the affirmation card saying, "I'm always prompt."

I don't know why I listened so intently, because I really didn't have that problem. I began reading the daily affirmation that was in our packet. I read The Power of Positive Thinking. *I've since read* Over the Top *twice and am working on my third time. I've also read four other books, and I had not read a single book in the last two years.*

In November, I bought your tapes on staying motivated, and I have listened to them at least ten times, and I plan on coming to "Born to Win" in February. There were some immediate and drastic changes. I began to come home on time. The kids, I have three, began to run to greet me instead of playing hide-and-seek and making me find them. My wife has even started to walk out and greet me. The kids ask me to start getting them up so that they can eat breakfast with me before I leave in the morning.

Michelle [his wife] started getting up earlier, and started having breakfast with us. These have been the best blessings, and they were unexpected. Michelle's support and encouragement has grown tenfold and is still growing. We set aside a day at the beginning of the year to identify family goals. It's a great meeting. We meet once a week to talk about our weekly goals.

My faith has improved dramatically. I weighed 230 pounds when I saw you in Dallas; I now weight 195. I drank five cups of coffee a day; now I drink a half or none each day. I had one or two candy bars and Cokes a day, and now I have none. I used to get two breakfast sandwiches at McDonald's; now I have cereal at home. I used to eat lunch out three to five times a week; now I take my lunch.

I'd always wanted to be comfortable in speaking to a group.

For four years he'd planned to get in Toastmasters. He finally did it when he was motivated to do it.

Results have been spectacular. I'd been trying to get in a regular exercise program for nine years. Before that I'd run twelve miles a week, but changing jobs, I allowed myself to get out of the habit with the excuse that it was not convenient. In those nine years, I'd gained forty pounds and four inches on my waist.

After hearing you, I started getting up an hour earlier. I'd tried this at least twenty-five times in the past and always reset my alarm. Now I get up when my opportunity clock goes off. I read Over the Top *for fifteen minutes, review my goals for fifteen minutes, and exercise for twenty minutes. I started off with five push-ups and twenty sit-ups and stretches. I'm now up to three sets of seventeen push-ups, three sets of fifty sit-ups, and my lower back hasn't felt this good since I was a teenager.*

I feel better, and everybody tells me I look better. My wife even told me I looked sexy, and she had never told me that before. Boy, you can bet that makes me feel good.

You see, when he changed, the wife and kids changed. That's the way you change other people. You change, they change. If they don't change, you learn to accept and understand them. That's important. Yes, with the motivation, you need instruction also.

I was a playground gladiator when I was a youngster. I used to fight everything that moved. I didn't care how big they were. I'm embarrassed to say how little they were. If I couldn't settle the argument in ten seconds or less, I'd just bust them one. That was the way I was.

A Mexican boy broke me of that habit. I've never been as glad to see a schoolteacher in my life. It took her all day to get there, but in my own defense, I will tell you this: I scared the poor guy half to death. He thought he had killed me.

Other than that, I was very successful on the playground, so in seventh grade, I decided I was going to go out for the boxing team. I weighed every bit of 82.5 pounds. I knew I was going to do good in that boxing ring. They had me sparring with a youngster who was 62.5 pounds. I felt so sorry for him. I knew this was going to be murder. I didn't realize he had been out for the boxing team for the last two years.

The bell sounded. We started round one. It took him nearly 3.5 seconds before he learned that the shortest distance to the end of my nose was a straight jab with his left. It took him another three seconds before he rediscovered that. I thought that kid had a bad memory, because he kept doing the same thing over and over and over. Before that round was over, I'd already decided that I was far too busy to go out for the boxing team.

Let me emphasize a point. When I stepped in the ring, I was optimistic, I was confident, I was enthusiastic, I was motivated, and I was getting killed. What am I saying? I'm saying that you can be motivated, but if you don't go to your golf pro and learn how to handle the swing, you're still going to have a lousy golf game. A doctor can be excited and enthused and motivated, but unless he goes to medical school, I don't want him working on anything inside of me, or outside of me.

The coach that day mercifully called an end to the match after one round, and then he started teaching me a little about defense. By the third day, I was able to keep from getting hit so much. By the end of two weeks, I was able to become the hitter instead of the hittee, and I quickly discovered that has a lot of benefits and advantages. By the end of the season, because of my extra weight, I was able to do better than just good.

Yes, motivation is important, but the motivation ought to lead to the education and training. That's the point I'm making.

If you're going to stay motivated, you need to develop a sense of humor. There's a little book called *Anguished English*. I encourage you to get it. It is the funniest thing I have encountered in I don't know when. Read it. It is absolutely hilarious.

Reader's Digest is one of my favorite sources. I love the story of this lady that was in this college town. She called her friend's son. She had been asked to do that, and she got his voice machine. The voice machine said, "If it's the telephone company calling, the check is in the mail. If it's the student-loan association, you should have made the loan bigger. If it's Mom, Mom, I am dead broke. Send me some money quick. If it's a girl, don't worry about money. I have plenty of it."

Why is humor so important? Researchers have found a connection between humor and family strength. Humorous remarks, family jokes, and a playful attitude were characteristics of a strong family and were found to be lacking in weaker families. A University of Michigan study concluded that people with a good sense of humor tend to be more creative, emotionally stable, realistic, and self-confident.

John Maxwell says, "A person who can laugh at life, laugh at himself, will have less stress in life. If you have a good sense of humor, you'll climb the ladder of success much faster. You build better relationships that help to generate team spirit."

I want to emphasize that when you're telling jokes, be very careful. No racist jokes, no sexist jokes. Don't start a joke that you cannot finish regardless of who is walking into the room. Filthy, violent language is just simply out of order. Humor, good, clean humor, is really one of the most uplifting things you can find.

Dr. Charles Allen sent out a fundraising letter under the guise of having had an incident happen. This gentleman had allegedly written him back and said:

> *In reply to your request to send a check, I wish to inform you that the present condition of my bank account makes it almost impossible. My shattered*

financial condition is due to federal laws, state, laws, county laws, corporation laws, in-laws, and outlaws. Through these taxes, I'm compelled to pay a business tax, amusement tax, head tax, school tax, gas tax, light tax, water tax, sales tax, and even my brains are taxed.

I'm required to get a business license, dog license, and marriage license while contributing to every organization that the society of man is capable of bringing to light. Comic relief, unemployment relief, every hospital and chapel and institution in the city, including the Red Cross, the Black Cross, the Purple Cross, and the double cross.

For my own safety, I'm required to carry life insurance, property insurance, liability insurance, burglar insurance, accident insurance, business insurance, earthquake insurance, tornado insurance, unemployment insurance, and fire insurance.

I'm inspected, expected, disrespected, rejected, dejected, examined, reexamined, informed, reformed, summoned, fined, commended, compelled until I provide an exhaustible supply of money for every known deed, desire, and hope of the human race. If I refuse to donate something or other, I'm boycotted, talked about, lied about, held up, held down, robbed until I am ruined.

I can tell you honestly that until the unexpected happened, I could not enclose this check.

The wolf that comes to so many doors nowadays, fortunately came to ours and just had pups in the kitchen. I've sold them, and here's the money.

A sense of humor helps. I was coming in on a plane once, and the flight attendant got on the intercom and said, "We are now making our final approach." Scared the wits out of me. I told her, "Quick, go tell the captain to make his next to final approach. I have some things I really want to get done."

You want to maintain that upbeat attitude. Take care of your health. Getting enough sleep is first on the list. When you burn the candle at both ends, it really inhibits that creativeness in your life. You're more prone to mistakes. You're not producing more. You simply are producing a different quality of work.

There's a difference between the workaholic and the peak performer. The workaholic works from fear and/or greed. It's easy to invest more hours in a job that you already enjoy and do well than it is to go on home and maybe face a rebellious child that you do not want to deal with. A peak performer works because of the love of what they're doing and their love of providing for their families.

Sleep deprivation has caused a lot of mistakes. We now know that the nuclear disaster at Three Mile Island was at least partially caused by people in important positions who had not had enough sleep and made critical mistakes because they did not have a trigger-sharp mind to handle the situation.

Chernobyl, beyond any doubt, was largely because of lack of sleep. The Challenger disaster, it is suspected, was at least partially because key people did not have the sharpness to make that critical, split-second decision that could have made a difference.

Without enough sleep, your energy level goes down. You're also more likely to become addicted not only to prescription drugs but to illegal drugs as well. The brain produces certain chemicals, and it can only do that during sleep. If you don't get enough sleep, it doesn't produce enough of those chemicals. The body demands balance, and that's when it happens. Your energy level goes down.

Number two, eat sensibly, and exercise regularly. Believe me, it does not take time. It will generate more time for you.

Then avoid the poisons, mainly tobacco and alcohol. There's been a lot of discussion about the fact that a drink a day will cut down on your heart attacks and you'll have less heart trouble, but the reality is that if you take one drink a day, chances are good that you're going to take the second one, and then the third one later, and then the fourth one. When you factor it all together, if we were to take 100 people that do not drink and say to them, "Start with a drink a day," and to another 100 we said, "Don't ever take a drink," the 100 who never took a drink would definitely have longer lifespans.

A lot of people say, "It relaxes me, it sharpens me up." Obviously you don't believe it sharpens you up.

If you believe that, will you insist that your surgeon have a little nip just before major surgery? I don't think so.

I've met a lot of people in my lifetime. I really have. Thus far I have never met a single human being that says, "You know, I have to tell you right now. Alcohol changed my life for the better." Not even once has that ever happened. I have seen the tragedy that happens when we do drink, and hear this. Many people become alcoholics with the first drink.

I've read countless stories of people fifty-five or sixty years old who took the first drink, and that lit the fire, and they immediately started drinking excessive amounts. We can tell you one out of nine to one out of eleven who take a social drink will end up with a drinking problem.

You've noticed throughout this book that I talk a lot about moral absolutes. There are a lot of people who talk about relative this and relative that. There really is no such thing.

I just got back in from Tampa, where I was in a golf tournament. When I got home, you know that redheaded wife of mine didn't ask me if I was *relatively* faithful to her. As a matter of fact, if I were relatively faithful to her, I'd be in big trouble. It wouldn't be relative trouble. It would be big trouble. There are some absolutes in life.

Think with me. All great failures are moral failures. What would have been the end result of history without those little character flaws of Richard Nixon or Spiro Agnew or Jim Wright or Bob Packwood or Mike Espy or Pete Rose or Gary Hart or Jimmy Swaggart or Jim Bakker? You see, there are some absolutes. All great failures are character failures. Check the records.

One of the things I'm most grateful for having the privilege of serving on the national board of advisors for the Boy Scouts of America. The Harris Poll was just completed a few months ago. Here's what they found. Of kids who served five years in the Scouts, 98 percent of them finished high school. What do they teach in the Scouts? "On my honor, I will do my best."

Then 40 percent of them finish college, versus 16 percent of the general population; 33 percent have incomes of over $50,000 a year, versus 17 percent of the general population; 70 percent of those kids who stay in Scouting five years end up in *Who's Who*; 72 percent of Rhodes Scholars were in Boy Scouts, and 94 percent of them said as adults that the character development they experienced when they were in the Scouts made a big difference in their character and values in their life. The good guys and the good gals really do win.

What does that bring us today? What are opportunities in America today? The choice is pretty much yours. Opportunity is either *now here* or *nowhere*. It depends on your attitude. The same letters, but they come out with an entirely different result. Opportunity really is now here, or it is nowhere, and the choice is up to you.

Again and again, 80 percent of all the millionaires in America are first-generation millionaires. Again, immigrants are four times as likely to become millionaires in America as are the people who are born here simply because they come and participate in the great dream.

You might say, "But, Zig, I worked hard all my life. I have those qualities. Nothing has happened."

Let me tell you a story. Jeff Hostetler is the starting quarterback for the Oakland Raiders. For the first four years he was in the league, he only had sixty-eight passes that he threw in regular season games. At the end of seven years, he had thrown under 200 passes. That's not exactly a very busy quarterback, because a quarterback generally throw thirty to fifty passes in one game.

Jeff Hostetler played for the New York Giants. He was the backup to Phil Simms. As most of us who are football fans know, when the Giants were playing in the Super Bowl, I think it was in about the eleventh game, Phil Simms went down. The coach turned to Jeff Hostetler, and he said, "OK, Jeff, it is your turn."

Jeff Hostetler picked up his helmet. He ran out on the field. He led the team to victory in that game, led them to the Super Bowl, led them to the World Championship. What would have happened if, when the coach said, "It's your turn, Jeff," he had said, "Wait a minute, coach, I have to get ready"?

Tomorrow when you show up for work, if your company were to say to you, "OK, it is your turn.

We are moving you up," would you be able to say, "I worked for this all of my life. I'm ready," or would you have to say, "Wait a minute, I have to get ready"?

What was Jeff Hostetler doing during those seven years? He lifted tons and tons of weights, ran thousands of wind sprints, jogged hour after hour developing that endurance. He threw thousands of passes through a moving target or at a moving target. He was at every practice session, every training campaign.

He was a team player supportive of his team. He was in on all of the offensive and defensive team. He was learning everything he could, and when the coach said, "It's your turn, Jeff," he was ready. That's what I'm really talking about getting ready.

Since 1989, according to *The Wall Street Journal*, 15 million new businesses have started, over half of them by women. They had some things in common. One, they had the great financial need. Two, they had virtually no skills. Three, they had no money.

Virtually all of them started what we call a *trust business,* meaning, "You give me the money, then I'll do the work," or "I will deliver the goods." There have been few, if any, prosecutions of women who did not deliver the goods. They had a great need for money, maybe because of a divorce or a husband who walked out on them, maybe because of downsizing or whatever, but they had a great need. Instead of saying, "Poor little me," they rolled up their sleeves and said, "Here's an opportunity for me to do something I have always wanted to do." They had gotten ready for it.

It is said that when Cicero spoke, the crowds would stand and cheer. When Demosthenes would speak, the crowds stood and marched. When the call comes for you to march toward the opportunity, toward getting the things in life that you really want, will you be ready, or will you have to say, "Wait a minute"?

Earlier I showed you a little diagram showing what appears to be sixteen squares. Then I pointed out that there were not sixteen squares, but when you look at all of them, there are thirty squares. But the reality is, when you really look at all of them and look at what you cannot see, there are literally hundreds and hundreds and hundreds of squares in it. It's infinity really.

I think a lot about people. What you see is not necessarily always what is there. Deep down inside, there is that incredible reserve. To motivate is to pull out or draw out. We've been talking about developing the qualities of success. You already have the seeds. We now need to develop them.

I'm going to conclude by simply sharing what I shared with you earlier. I'm going to share with you what the top really is. This time, you're probably wondering why I'm repeating it. This time, I'm putting it in the first person, present tense.

When I put my name in it, that's where you want to put your name in it.

I, Zig Ziglar, am at the top because I understand that failure is an event, not a person, that yesterday ended last night, and today is my brand-new day. I'm at the top because I've made friends with my past, am focused on the present, and optimistic about my future.

I am at the top because I know that success, a win, doesn't make me, and failure, a loss, doesn't break me. I am at the top because I am filled with faith, hope, and love and live without anger, greed, guilt, envy, or thoughts of revenge.

I, Zig Ziglar, am at the top because I am mature enough to delay gratification and shift my focus from my rights to my responsibilities. I am at the top because I know that failure to stand for what is morally right is the prelude to being the victim of what is criminally wrong. I am at the top because I am secure in who I am so I am at peace with God and in fellowship with man. I am at the top because I made friends of my adversaries and have gained the love and respect of those who know me best.

I, Zig Ziglar, am at the top because I understand that others can give me pleasure, but genuine happiness comes when I do things for others. I am at the top because I am pleasant to the grouch, courteous to the rude, and generous to the needy. I am at the top because I love the unlovable, give hope to the hopeless, friendship to the friendless, and encouragement to the discouraged.

I am at the top because I look back in forgiveness, forward in hope, down in compassion, and up with gratitude. I am at the top because I know that he who would be the greatest among you must become the servant of all. I am at the top because I recognize, confess, develop, and use my God-given physical, mental, and spiritual abilities to the glory of God and for the benefit of mankind.

I, Zig Ziglar, will be over the top when I stand in front of the creator of the universe and He says to me, "Well done, thou good and faithful servant."

I encourage you to take these one at a time. Make it a weekly objective. Read it, memorize it, keep it in front of you, claim it, and you'll be astonished at what will happen to you, your life, your family, your friends, and the people who know you.

Buy the ideas we've talked about. Follow through on these procedures, because if you do, I will see you, and yes, I really do mean you, not just at the top—I'm going to see you over the top.